THE SIXTH KING

Rise of the Antichrist within the New World Order

DAVID BRENNAN, SR.

The Sixth King

Website for this book: www.SwordofDavid.com

Published by Teknon Publishing, Covington, Louisiana

ISBN: 978-1-7324135-2-8

Retailers and distributors qualify for special discounts on bulk purchases. For more information, email Teknon Publishing at:

SwordofDavid@Yahoo.com

To Jesus Christ, the Son of the living God.
Who brought salvation and hope to a world in need.

Contents

PART IV: CONQUERING AMERICA

PART V: ABILITIES AND METHODS OF THE ANTICHRIST

PART I
THE NEW WORLD ORDER IS THE BEAST KINGDOM

Chapter One

THE TIME HAS ARRIVED

There is a growing sense within the church and conservative political circles of an evil power operating in the world today. An unseen force moving behind the scenes and whose control appears to have grown dramatically in recent years. A power that uniquely focuses on driving America and the world into spiritual darkness. A blackness of which has never before been seen. *The Sixth King* presents the case that those observations are nothing more than the outward signs of the presence of a new dark kingdom that now exists on the earth. One spoken of by the prophets. And that its coming leader, the Antichrist, is almost certainly actively engaging the world.

The Bible tells us there is a world leader coming who will succeed in destroying on a global scale and to a degree unplumbed by the worst before him. He has many names in Scripture. Some of these are the "vile person," "the Assyrian," "the beast," and "the man of sin." But the most popular one is that of the Antichrist. Although we are told in Scripture that anyone who denies Jesus as Christ is a form of antichrist, an actual evil individual is coming to rule the world; he will be the Antichrist.

As for his kingdom, the details are many, and they create a picture that increasingly resembles the borderless entity that today has taken on the popular name of the New World Order. A dark modern-day entity that appears to have organized in secret over the course of time to exert great power and influence worldwide. A hidden kingdom that appears to have control over a multitude of leaders who do its bidding. A kingdom whose dark tentacles appear to be embedded within the most powerful institutions across the world. Especially in the West. A force that appears to be driving nations entangled in its dark web to fulfill a twisted will. In fact, it appears to have reached a level of power that enables it to move whole societies in the direction of Satan. To such a degree that it qualifies as the long-awaited Biblical Beast Kingdom.

The prophet Daniel described the Beast Kingdom as one that would be "diverse" or "different" from all kingdoms before it. And what currently exists as the New World Order qualifies on that score like no other kingdom in world history. It is a borderless world kingdom with massive power to manipulate nation-states that are within its grip. And those most entangled appear to be Western nations, especially the United States. As the leader of the West, the United States seems to have received special attention. And the worldwide signs that the Beast Kingdom has metastasized into its dark fullness abound. Especially within America.

In recent years, the United States has suddenly and rapidly been transformed into a nation where men can "marry" men, and women can "marry" women. A nation where one of the central questions of the day is how many genders there are. As well as if a 10-year-old can do irreparable damage to their sexual organs. A nation where men can use the women's bathroom and those who object are the ones receiving condemnation. And where satanic ceremonies are now openly practiced on nationwide TV. In many cases, those leading the way are college students demonstrating all the characteristics of dark indoctrination instead of education. Not only has America been leading the Western set of nations in these cultural directions, but it has also been in a rush toward World War III. All of this being accelerated dramatically by a "puppet president" and raising one of the questions addressed in this book: "Who is really running America?"

In addition to the goal of gaining total control over the finances, lives, and minds of persons within these nations, the New World Order appears to have the single-minded goal of driving them into becoming forms of a Satanic theocracy. Where satanic ritual abuse of children is now widespread. Turning them into nations where good is called evil and evil is called good. A complete renunciation of basic Christian beliefs. A very "different" kind of kingdom. It is also an ultra-secret kingdom. A hidden kingdom written about by President Woodrow Wilson in the year 1913. A hidden kingdom that allowed a professor to study it for two years back in the 1960s. A hidden kingdom spoken about by General Douglas MacArthur, British Prime Minister Benjamin Disraeli, U.S. Senators, one of the world's most powerful bankers, David Rockefeller, and other notable persons.[1]

The church should not find it strange that the prince of darkness would develop his earthly end time kingdom in the shadows, hidden from direct viewing. Satan and his minions prefer to dwell in that place. And this New World Order entity has grown into a monolith in the realm of darkness. A hidden kingdom that appears to have likely attained its final Biblical ruling structure sometime around the year 1900. The case of which will be presented. And although the church has been aware of the rise of the New World Order, it missed the great significance of what it meant. It is a massively powerful dark kingdom that is the most "diverse" or "different" in world history.[2] Just as Daniel told us to look for!

In America and the West, the New World Order appears to have made the greatest inroads, moving nations from freedom toward a beastly form of totalitarianism. Controlling major media corporations by filling them with like-minded individuals — indoctrinated in darkness at "universities"— many who appear to have transitioned from educational institutions into dark seminaries long ago. Australia and Canada represent two of the most deplorable examples. Both nations are becoming pacesetters in moving their populations toward totalitarianism.[3, 4]

And there is the strange rise of Barack Hussein Obama to consider. His managed ascension to power in addition to his ghastly deeds as President indicating when America came almost completely under the control of this dark kingdom. Except for some notable power centers still resisting. It is the hidden kingdom that rules nations from within. Leading to the disturbing conclusion that America is far along the road of being completely conquered. Becoming one of many nations either conquered from within or very close to it. This explains why there are now so many brazenly open appeals to darkness taking place. Even satanic ceremonies enacted on nationwide TV during such events as the Grammy Awards.

When considering the details of Obama's rise to the presidency, there is a litany of tell-tale signs of an ultra-powerful hidden hand moving behind the scenes to elevate him from one political office to the next. Signs that all point to the New World Order. With such an ungodly entity guiding his rise, we can understand why it was so important for him to openly oppose Christianity at every turn. Even announcing that America was no longer a Christian nation.[5] An otherwise odd statement from a national leader and one that must have echoed loudly in the spirit realm. And why he found it necessary to light up the White House in the rainbow colors of homosexuality. As well as engaging in countless other anti-Christian deeds done quietly behind the scenes. A man simply fulfilling the will of the entity that placed him in power. It also explains why every strong tentacle of the Beast Kingdom went insane when Donald Trump won the presidency in 2016. An unexpected victory that temporarily ripped its crown jewel, the United States, out of its grip. And in its rage, it made certain such an outcome wouldn't happen again in the 2020 election.

It is also no wonder the 2020 election that replaced Trump was the shadiest in U.S. history. Leaving many wondering if the man who won the election is the one not residing in the White House. It also explains why the man chosen to replace Trump, Joe Biden, appears to be nothing more than a puppet leader. A widespread observation embraced for the first time in U.S. history by many Americans. But one thing is certain: Based on Mr. Biden's actions, he is a New World Order man. This also explains why it appears he isn't making any decisions. Because he isn't. Perfectly fulfilling the perspective of this book.

Antichrist Prophecy Verses

From a scriptural perspective, there are certain prophecy verses relating to the Antichrist that are best resolved by viewing the rise of the New World Order as the rise of the Biblical Beast Kingdom. One such question is found in Daniel 8. In verses 11 and 12, we are told about the Antichrist stopping the revived Jewish sacrifice at their new temple. But to do so, he must be "given" a "host" (army).

> [12] And a host (army) was given him against the daily sacrifice by reason of transgression, and it cast down the truth to the ground, and it practiced, and prospered. Daniel 8

We are told the Antichrist must be "given" an army to take the city of Jerusalem and stop the Jewish sacrifices. This is no minor point. The word "given" is the Hebrew verb "natan." Which means to give, bestow or grant. A literal reading tells us that he must be "given" an army. And this implies he doesn't have his own army at that point. This fits well with the thesis of this book. Because the New World Order does not have its own army. But uses the armies of the nations it controls. It is the most powerful kingdom on earth today. Yet, it is not possible to identify an army it calls its own. In Revelation 6, another verse plays to the same point. Wherein the Antichrist has a "bow" as he goes about "conquering." But no arrows!

> [2] And I saw, and behold a white horse: and he that sat on him had a bow, and a crown was given unto him: and he went forth conquering, and to conquer. Revelation 6

The rider of the "white horse" is the Antichrist. But notice he only has a "bow" but no arrows. A "bow" is used to direct an attack. Whereas an arrow is an attack. This is because no arrows come directly from him. Yet, the verse tells us, "he went forth conquering, and to conquer." This is fully in line with his needing to be given a "host" (army) in Daniel 8 to take Jerusalem.

The same answer resolves both verses. The "diverse" or "different" kingdom Daniel warned us of is the borderless one we currently call the New World Order. It is a hidden kingdom that controls nations from the shadows. And there has never before been an entity as powerful in all of history. However, by its nature of being a hidden force — manipulating nations under its control to do its will — it does not have its own army. This is why, for the Antichrist to have the honor of capturing Jerusalem, he must be "given" an army from one of his vassal nation-states. This also explains why, as he goes about "conquering" in Revelation 6, he only has a "bow" but no arrows. His "bow" directs the arrows (armies) of the nations under his control. And he does not receive blame for those wars from such a hidden place. While at the same time, he has the control ("bow") to end the wars. And this bestows upon him the mantel of peacemaker. Even though he is ultimately the one behind the wars. The man is incredibly deceptive, having perfected "dark sentences" and "craft" to a degree that the world has never before seen. Because of the "diverse" or "different" nature of the Beast Kingdom, he looks like a "Peace" maker even though he is a monster.

Ten Kingdoms

Within the church, there are various perspectives on certain prophecy Scriptures. And this should not be cause for division. Sincere and dedicated students of Bible prophecy occasionally come to different conclusions. But if the rise of this New World Order is the much-anticipated

Beast Kingdom, then it has been missed due to a certain perspective that has been widely embraced. That perspective is that the Antichrist comes out of a ten-kingdom confederacy of some kind. This author embraced that concept for thirty years. And, as a result of that teaching, since there is currently no such grouping of powerful nations, it would mean that the Beast Kingdom does not yet exist. Causing many in the church to miss the fact that it has already risen. With the Antichrist now very close to his throne! Multiple signs present themselves that this is the case, which will be covered in detail.

That there will be a ten-kingdom confederacy associated with the rule of the Antichrist is a solid scriptural fact found in the Books of Daniel and Revelation. It will exist. However, the case will be presented that this dark confederacy comes into existence only <u>after</u> the Antichrist rises to the throne of the Beast Kingdom. The scriptural case will be presented that the Beast Kingdom begins as a single, very powerful, borderless kingdom. "Diverse" or "different," just as Daniel said it would be. Only later adding the ten kingdoms. It will also be presented that the New World Order/Beast Kingdom has developed in stages over a period of decades. And although elements of it have certainly existed for a very long time, it will be presented that only around the year 1900 did it finally assume its Biblically indicated form. With such an orderly ruling structure, it was then able to assume greater and greater control over the affairs of nations from its hidden seat of power. Power that has expanded exponentially in recent years. And that the progression of this control has now reached its fullness, with its minions currently filling the most powerful seats of control, especially throughout the West. Thanks in large part to Mr. Biden. A president prepared to relinquish vast amounts of American sovereignty to the United Nations. A template for the one-world government.

The conclusion that the ten kingdoms do not come into existence until after the Antichrist rises to the throne is the result of taking various Scriptures very literally. And this conclusion opens the door wide to the New World Order being the prophesied Beast Kingdom. With an array of additional prophecies ready to trigger the beginning of the violent end times. There is also a seldom-quoted verse in Isaiah that will be reviewed. One that literally has the Antichrist telling us something of great importance about these ten kings. A detail that helps place them in the proper context of what they are before they become actual kings.

It should also be considered that if the ten-kingdom confederacy must first exist before the Antichrist can rise to power — and yet it is nowhere to be found on the political horizon — then the end times cannot be close to starting. Even as the New World Order is rapidly checking each of the boxes of the foretold Beast Kingdom. And also, as the times beckon the church, the season is here.

The Sixth King

Additionally, *The Sixth King* will present the scriptural case that there is a clear succession of Beast Kingdom leaders — referred to in Scripture as kings — and that the Antichrist will be its sixth king. (And also the eighth due to assassination!) Once it is understood that the Beast Kingdom starts as a single entity, only later morphing to add the ten kingdoms, and that its Biblical ruling structure has existed for decades, the succession of kings leading to the Antichrist becomes clear. Knowing that there will only be five beast kings before the Antichrist is of critical importance as well. Because it tells us something about the ruling structure of the New World Order/Beast Kingdom. That it reaches its final Biblical form only decades before the Antichrist rises to the throne. (That is not to say elements of it did not exist long before.) This also opens the door to something else. That the New World Order/Beast Kingdom has matured to the point that the Antichrist — the sixth king — must be getting very close to assuming the throne. In fact, for the first time, three signposts support this.

One signpost occurred in the early 1900s, when a seminal financial event occurred. That event appears to indicate the rough time frame wherein the New World Order/Beast Kingdom reached a level of organized power, indicating it had finally attained the ruling structure indicated in Scripture. Adding further evidence that the Antichrist is very close to power since there can only be five kings before him. The second signpost is an event that took place in recent years. One that appears to have all the tell-tale signs that the Antichrist is actively on the scene. An event that implemented the most brilliant and vastly dark plan ever devised in world history. A gambit that sidestepped the legal structures of Western "democracies" and literally moved the world toward a global police state. The whole event representing a clear sign that the "dark sentences" and intrigues the Antichrist has mastery of have finally arrived. Indicating how close he must now be to assuming the throne of the satanic kingdom.

And the final indication of the nearness of the Antichrist taking the Beast throne is the progression of control by the New World Order/Beast Kingdom in the affairs of nations. Keeping up with the degree of control Scripture assures us the dark kingdom will possess. Control that now extends to every important power center, especially in the West. Including technological advances that enable massive control over individuals to a degree never before imagined. With such control, federal law enforcement agencies such as the F.B.I. and the Department of Justice have been transformed into authoritarian threats to traditional-thinking Americans. And with the coming-of-age of artificial intelligence, the power of the New World Order has been amplified as never before.

And there is the coming to life of Revelation 13. With the implementation of a rapidly evolving structure of total control. Control over the citizens of the world to a degree never before imagined. Ready for the "man of sin" to begin using. The stage is now set for the curtain to rise. With multiple factors pointing to the nearness of the Antichrist taking the throne.

Chapter Two

THE NEW WORLD ORDER

… and power was given him over all kindreds,
and tongues, and nations.

REVELATION 13

The year is 1913, and the "war to end all wars" will start in just twelve short months. Thrusting the flower of European youth into a grinder of fire and steel that will be called the First World War. Death on an unthinkable scale is about to envelope them thanks to advancements in killing technology. Bringing death and destruction to tens of millions of people on a continental scale. On the other side of the Atlantic, Americans are living their lives without a thought of engaging in the affairs of Europe. And there is a new American president in the White House: Woodrow Wilson, who, in the first year of his presidency, is publishing his book *The New Freedom*.

In it, Wilson presents his vision for an America of great opportunity for all of its citizens. A future that beckons all Americans, regardless of their race or religious beliefs. But there is a strange statement within the pages of his book. A confession of sorts that stands out like a sore thumb. The President acknowledges something that Americans had wondered about since Andrew Jackson killed the Second Bank of the United States and was then almost assassinated. Jackson feared too much power was flowing to unknown and unaccountable forces over the affairs of the nation through the central bank. Now Wilson identifies the evolving entity that opposed Jackson in that great political battle. Writing openly about the power and influence it possesses over the affairs of nations. A force so powerful and hidden that even the most powerful men in America dare not speak above their low breath in condemnation of it.

> "Since I have entered politics, I have chiefly had men's views confided to me privately. Some of the biggest men in the U.S., in the field of commerce and manufacturing, are afraid of somebody, are afraid of something. They know that there is a power somewhere so organized, so subtle, so watchful, so interlocked, so complete, so persuasive, that they had better not speak above their breath when they speak in condemnation of it."[1]

Ironically, it would be Wilson — the President who acknowledged the dark and powerful force working behind the scenes — who would reinstitute the threat of a national bank. But on a scale vastly greater and more intrusive than Jackson's worst fears. The Federal Reserve System. Placing control over the issuance of money in the United States directly into the hands of a powerful few.

In describing this entity, Wilson chose his words with great care. Specifically detailing the strength and depth of this unseen force at play in the affairs of the nation. A force so undemocratic as to stamp VOID upon any democracy so entangled. He speaks of this power as coming from "somewhere." But does not tell us from where. Although one would suspect that he knew. But he chose not to cross that particular line. Then he begins describing its grip on power in terms typically reserved for dictatorial entities.

He describes it as so "organized" and yet so "subtle." In other words, it is hidden in the shadows. In line with its very "organized" nature, it is "interlocked" and "complete." It is not only "watchful" but also "persuasive." It is capable of making even the most powerful enact its will. But there is one description that requires special attention. Ominously, he is telling us that back in 1913, it was "complete." Indicating that at that time it possessed an organized structure, making it fundamentally "complete" as an entity.

There is no speculation here. Those are his words, indicating that this all-powerful yet "subtle" entity was "complete" back in the year 1913. And well "organized" at that time as well. Indicating its ruling structure was in place and engaging in the exercise of its considerable power sometime before the year 1913. But it would also appear to be international for a simple reason.

This force Wilson describes is not controlled by "the biggest men in the U.S., in the field of commerce and manufacturing." In fact, they "are afraid of somebody, are afraid of something." It is difficult to imagine such powerful industrial leaders, as described by Wilson, being afraid of anything. It was they who were the power titans within the borders of the U.S. With their wealth and connections, such people are typically the untouchables. But whatever this hidden entity is, it caused fear in the hearts of the most powerful leaders within the United States. And this appears to make it something from outside the United States. International.

Perhaps the most notable feature Wilson describes may explain why the prophet Daniel warned us that the Beast Kingdom would be different from all kingdoms before it. Wilson describes it as "subtle." Why would it operate so subtly? Because of its basic nature. It is an entity dedicated to undermining the sovereignty of nations from within. So its existence and goals must remain hidden. Those allied with it must not be exposed.

Wilson would not be the only notable American who would openly acknowledge the existence of a hidden force moving behind the scenes. A multitude of others would as well. General Douglas MacArthur would be quoted as saying, "I am concerned for the security of our great Nation;

not so much because of any threat from without, but because of the insidious forces working from within."[2] Former F.B.I. Director J. Edger Hoover — a man with the best sources for information — revealed the unbelievable nature of what he was seeing. Stating that "The individual is handicapped by coming face-to-face with a conspiracy so monstrous he cannot believe it exists."[3] Two former U.S. Senators would add their voices to these warnings.

Former 1964 presidential candidate Senator Barry Goldwater observed and revealed a hidden power working behind the scenes. "The Trilateralist Commission is international...(and)...is intended to be the vehicle for multinational consolidation of the commercial and banking interests by seizing control of the political government of the United States. The Trilateralist Commission represents a skillful, coordinated effort to seize control and consolidate the four centers of power - political, monetary, intellectual, and ecclesiastical."[4] A warning, and that is exactly what has happened since he delivered it!

Years later, another senator heading a committee investigating the Central Intelligence Agency (CIA) would speak about a "shadowy government" operating behind a cloak of darkness. Pointing out it has "its own Air Force, its own Navy, its own fundraising mechanism, and the ability to pursue its own ideas of the national interest, free from all checks and balances, and free from the law itself."[5]

It has not been just big-name people who see an ultra-powerful force acting behind the scenes. But more and more of the American people see an evil force altering the religious beliefs of the nation to create fertile ground for a new dark moral order to take hold. A process lasting only decades. Speeded up greatly by the advent of mass communication technology. Directing people toward a satanic system of beliefs and away from Christian morals. Modern-day America and Western Europe are testaments to their success. And that this has happened reflects on two goals of this entity. Not only the attainment of absolute power. But driving nations into the grip of satanic beliefs. Both goals of the Biblical Beast Kingdom.

A man who revealed the satanic side of the New World Order was spiritualist David Spangler. As a well-connected and influential American spiritual philosopher and self-described "practical mystic," Spangler would point out: "No one will enter the New World Order unless he or she pledges to worship Lucifer. No one will enter the New Age unless he will take a Luciferian Initiation."[6] Not coincidentally, Satanism has been on the rise in the West in recent years. Of course, we know from Revelation 13 that such an open satanic acknowledgment will one day be necessary to buy and sell.

Although Wilson would reveal the existence of this secret and ultra-powerful cabal working behind the scenes, it would be his administration that would provide a great leap forward for it. The man who warned about a secret cabal would himself promote the creation of the League of Nations. An international group of the most powerful European countries to create a structure for nations to openly give up their sovereignty for a stated benefit. In this case, collective security. A worthy cause. But also a group representing the first step in a move toward a one-world government in fulfillment of Biblical prophecy. Wilson would fail in his efforts to include the United States in the new organization. Rebuffed by a U.S. Senate that feared American sovereignty would be compromised. The senators remembered Washington's warning against becoming entangled in a network involving other nations. And for good reason.

But Wilson would find success elsewhere in his drive for internationalism. And it would mainly come from the efforts of one of his closest advisors, Col. Edward House. A true internationalist "one-world government" type. House's beliefs included the promotion of "socialism as dreamed of by Karl Marx," articulated in his book, *Phillip Dru: Administrator,* published in 1912.[7] Of course, the essence of Marx's socialist beliefs was that of a worldwide worker's paradise where God played no public role. A one-world government kind of paradise. But House's efforts went far beyond just words in a book.

In the year 1913, House was part of a powerful group of bankers and politicians meeting at Jekyll Island, Georgia. The purpose of the meeting was to plot the transfer of money creation from the federal government to a group of private bankers. With the support of the Wilson Administration, the cabal birthed the Federal Reserve System with passage of the Federal Reserve Act in November 1913. A central bank. Ultimately, evolving into the coordinator of central banks around the world. Representing the genesis of a one-world banking system. An essential entity in implementing total control over money to the extent that buying and selling can be controlled centrally, fulfilling Revelation 13:17: "And that no man might buy or sell, save he that had the mark, or the name of the beast, or the number of his name."

Ironically, the Federal Reserve would be created in the same year Wilson would publish his book revealing the existence of the powerful hidden entity. Leading one to wonder if his statement in the book was a pang of conscience, knowing he would later succumb to the will of that same entity. Turning over the creation of money to a group of private bankers. Essentially, turning over the economy and stock market to them. Both empowering and enriching them to an unimaginable extent. As a former college professor, Wilson was naive. Later expressing his regret at turning over such power to so few. According to Wilson, he was "a most unhappy man. I have unwittingly ruined my country. A great industrial nation is controlled by its system of credit. Our system of credit is concentrated. The growth of the nation, therefore, and all our activities are in the hands of a few men." But by the time that realization dawned on him, it was too late. But this whole affair of granting massive financial power to a few individuals deserves more consideration. Consideration that involve real life power politics at the highest level.

We know that Col. House organized the Jekyll Island meeting in the first year of Wilson's Administration. And of all the initiatives a new administration can embark upon, this was apparently at the top of House's list and not Wilson's. That conclusion is reasonable because

Wilson later expressed great regret at the whole affair. And expressing such extreme regrets in writing after the fact likely means he had reservations all along. So it is fair to conclude that Col. House was the real driving force behind the Federal Reserve being established, and that it was his top priority to be addressed in Wilson's first year in office. What we do not know is what powerful forces placed Col. House in such a strategic position within Wilson's Administration. But such positions as Col. House found himself in are coveted and require the help of very powerful friends. Whatever force was behind him had to be very powerful. All of this happening within the administration of a president who wrote about a powerful entity working behind the scenes. The entity that placed Col. House in his position?

After centralizing the power of money creation into the hands of a powerful few, Col. House would work toward moving U.S. foreign policy in the same direction. In 1919, along with prominent British and American individuals, he would establish the Royal Institute of International Affairs in England and the Institute of International Affairs in the U.S. Just two years later, the Institute of International Affairs was reorganized into the Council on Foreign Relations. The CFR. All the way back in 1922, it endorsed a world government in its *Foreign Affairs* magazine. The first truly organized effort toward a one-world government had begun. Thanks in large part to the efforts of Col. House. The same man whom played a major part in establishing the Federal Reserve. The New World Order could not have asked for a better man.

As the decades passed and the CFR grew in power, its support became essential for individuals seeking high-level foreign policy positions in the U.S. and overseas. Effectively, stacking the deck with cards that all read "one-world government." As a non-partisan organization, it supports individuals that promote its policies of one-world government regardless of party affiliation. And once appointed, its members appear to faithfully follow the tenants of the organization. The key tenant being the relinquishing of national sovereignty for the greater good as determined by the organization. Leading CFR member and statesman of his time, Henry Kissinger, concerning the CFR, would add that the organization "believes national boundaries should be obliterated and one-world rule established."[8] And the grandest success for those seeking a one-world government would come in the year 1945.

The Government of All Nations

Great crises present great opportunities for those who wish to take advantage of them. And the Second World War was the greatest crisis since Europe was invaded by the Ottoman Empire in 1683. Immediately after the defeat of Nazi Germany and its allies, the world quickly organized itself into the United Nations. And for the first time in human history, there existed on earth an organization representing "all nations." Impossible to achieve without the steady influence of one-world government organizations that filled governments in the West with their allies. That very "organized, so subtle, so watchful, so interlocked, so complete, so persuasive" entity Wilson wrote about had just changed the world. Without as much as one of its leaders being openly known!

All Nations

Although most students of Bible prophecy understand the significance of the rebirth of the state of Israel that happened three years later in 1948, there is also notable significance in the creation of the United Nations. Just as the end times could not start without the reappearance of Israel as foretold by the prophets, so, too, is the case for the existence of an entity representing "all nations." (The Valley of Dry Bones prophecy of Israel's return.) The reason why is noted by the prophets. In addition to being a forerunner of a coming one-world government, "all nations" fulfill another critical prophetic role.

Various prophets describe monolithic end time events involving an entity referred to by them as "all nations." Joel and Jeremiah directly speak to it. Paul and Daniel indirectly. Until the birth of the United Nations, it was difficult to envision an entity that could act on behalf of "all nations." But no more. Consider the following Scripture describing events centered on "all nations" from the Book of Joel.

In the Book of Joel, chapter 2, the prophet begins describing the launch of "the day of the Lord"—the time of God unleashing His wrath against the world. Starting in verse 30, he tells of certain unique signs that will take place before it begins.

> [30]And I will shew wonders in the heavens and in the earth, blood, and fire, and pillars of smoke. [31]The sun shall be turned into darkness, and the moon into blood, before the great and terrible day of the Lord come. Joel 2:30-31

Before "the day of the Lord" begins, we are told of a war on the earth that will be associated with some kind of "wonders in the heavens" as a positive identifier of that war. Then we are told of another great sign that will play out involving the sun and the moon. However, it is two verses later that Joel includes "all nations" in the picture.

> [2]I will also gather all nations, and will bring them down into the valley of Jehoshaphat, and will plead with them there for my people and for my heritage Israel, whom they have scattered among the nations, and parted my land. Joel 3:2

We are told "all nations" are being punished in the valley of Jehoshaphat — the theater of God's judgment against the nations of the world. And then we are told why they are being punished. They "parted my land"—the land of Israel. For having parted the land of Israel, "all nations" face punishment in the "valley of Jehoshaphat." And thus, an entity representing "all nations" was always necessary to fulfill an important end time role. But it has other roles as well. It is a prototype for world government.

> And it was given unto him to make war with the saints, and to overcome them: <u>and power was given him over all kindreds, and tongues, and nations</u>. Revelation 13

And...

> [23]Thus he said, The fourth beast shall be the fourth kingdom upon earth, which shall be diverse from all kingdoms, <u>and shall devour the whole earth</u>, and shall tread it down, and break it in pieces. Daniel 7

The birth of the United Nations took an important step toward the fulfillment of both Scriptures foretelling a worldwide kingdom that would one day rule with an evil rod. Revelation 13 tells us that the Beast Kingdom led by the Antichrist will have power "over all kindreds, and tongues, and nations." And Daniel tells us his power will be so great that he "shall devour the whole earth, tread it down, and break it to pieces." This accomplishment of finally creating an entity that represents "all nations" is ultimately owed to the Wilson Administration. Empowering the one-world government group led by Col. House to get the United States on the same page as its European counterparts. The same administration that gave control over the nation's money supply to a small, powerful group of men. The same president who revealed the existence of the ultra-powerful hidden entity moving behind the scenes. The entity popularly referred to today as the New World Order.

Wilson's Dark Entity

The entity Wilson and others wrote about has allowed itself to be studied. Professor Carroll Quigley, President Bill Clinton's mentor at Georgetown University, states that he was allowed two years to study the papers and secret documents of this powerful entity. No doubt, it's the same one President Wilson wrote about years earlier. Still operating as subtly as it did in Wilson's day. About it, he writes:

> "I know of the operations of this network [the Round Table Groups] because I have studied it for twenty years and was permitted for two years, in the early 1960s, to examine its papers and secret records. I have no aversion to it or to most of its aims and have, for much of my life, been close to it and to many of its instruments. I have objected, both in the past and recently, to a few of its policies, but in general my chief difference of opinion is that it wishes to remain unknown, and I believe its role in history is significant enough to be known."[9]

According to Quigley back in the 1960s, this secret cabal's "role in history is significant enough [for it] to be known." In other words, he was able to observe that it has had a significant historical impact. Quigley was allowed to study its "secret records." He agreed with its goals. And the only real issue he had with it was "that it wishes to remain unknown." No doubt, what Quigley studied was a more evolved version of what Wilson wrote about.

Having had access to the secret records of the secret entity, Quigley would reveal one of its goals in his 1965 book *Tragedy and Hope*. A goal so grand as to boggle the mind of the average citizen. Just as the late F.B.I. director J. Edgar Hoover said would be the case. A goal perfectly in line with the actions of both Wilson and House in 1913. Possibly explaining why Wilson felt the need to openly and in broad terms describe the existence of the ultra-powerful and hidden international entity moving behind the scenes to alter the course of nations. A hidden kingdom.

According to Quigley, that goal was "to create a world system of financial control in private hands able to dominate the political system of each country and the economy of the world." Going on to note that the "growth of financial capitalism made possible a centralization of world economic control and use of this power for the direct benefit of financiers and direct injury of all other economic groups."[10] Those are the words of the man allowed to study its secret documents and record of achievements. All of this places in context plans for the introduction by the central bankers of a Central Bank Digital Currency (CBDC) into the Western financial system.

Such complete financial control is the noose that has been tied around the financial necks of nations across the world over the last several decades. Achieving one of its goals identified by Quigley. Empowering this small group to direct the economic lives of nations with an absoluteness that was never before possible. Wrestling total financial control over the United States away from the people. And within the United States, the beginning of that control was gained in 1913 with the creation of the Federal Reserve. An entity created by the president, who slightly lifted the rock under which the hidden kingdom could be found.

Associated with this powerful but secret entity, international organizations sprang up. With the massive financial power it attained in 1913, the world became its oyster. Using its newly attained power, it moved rapidly to create international organizations that would serve and promote its goals of a one-world government. Organizations that successfully burrowed deep into the power structures of nations, especially the Western block of nations. Further expanding the power of the hidden kingdom. A good example of such an organization is the Rockefeller Brothers Fund.

Controlled by the ultra-wealthy Rockefeller family, it is an organization intimately associated with promoting a one-world government. From that organization, a paper was published titled: *The Mid-Century Challenge to U.S. Foreign Policy*. In it, a certain all-encompassing goal of this hidden entity was revealed.

> "...cannot escape, and indeed should welcome...the task which history has imposed on us. This is the task of helping to shape a new world order in all its dimensions—spiritual, economic, political, social."[11]

The open acknowledgment of efforts to reshape the entire world "in all its dimensions" truly represents a "new world order." One where not only the financial and economic spheres are under complete control but, most ominously, the "spiritual" as well. But why the "spiritual"? If this hidden kingdom was simply a group seeking great wealth and power, then the spiritual part should not be that appealing. Guaranteed to only complicate their efforts. Unless there was a deeper meaning behind it all. Perhaps Luciferian worship, as noted by the spiritualist David Spangler. And written about by the prophets long ago concerning the beastly nature of the Antichrist's kingdom. A dark kingdom destined to not only attain complete financial and economic control but also seek the souls of men through spiritual control. Total financial control, where even buying and selling are governed by a person's spiritual acknowledgments.

This hidden kingdom has been seen internationally by notable leaders in Europe. One was the late Benjamin Disraeli, former Prime Minister and one of the greatest British statesmen of all time. Who observed the hidden entity in the following terms:

> "The governments of the present day have to deal not merely with other governments, with emperors, kings

and ministers, but also with the secret societies which have everywhere their unscrupulous agents, and can at the last moment upset all the governments' plans.

...The world is governed by very different personages from what is imagined by those who are not behind the scenes."[12]

Disraeli described a world ruled by people "behind the scenes." By "secret societies" that have "everywhere their unscrupulous agents." He wrote this in the mid-1800s. Years before the hidden kingdom would grow into the powerful, dark monolith it is today. Likely, what Disraeli saw was the less organized branches of the same entity that years later would be identified by Wilson.

Some of the most powerful men to have walked the earth come from ultra-wealthy families. Next to the Rothschild banking family in Europe, John D. Rockefeller built an unimaginable fortune at the turn of the last century. A fortune inherited by his children, one of whom was his son, David Rockefeller. As chairman of Chase Manhattan Bank in New York and with his family's massive wealth and contacts, when Mr. Rockefeller spoke, the wise listened.

"Some even believe we (the Rockefeller family) are part of a secret cabal working against the best interests of the United States, characterizing my family and me as 'internationalists' and of conspiring with others around the world to build a more integrated global political and economic structure—one world, if you will. If that's the charge, I stand guilty, and I am proud of it."[13]

And how has such a plot and direct statement by one of the world's most powerful persons gone unreported? Statements that should have roused the public to defend their nation and freedom? Mr. Rockefeller addressed that as well.

> "We are grateful to the Washington Post, the New York Times, Time Magazine, and other great publications whose directors have attended our meetings and respected their promises of discretion for almost 40 years. It would have been impossible for us to develop our plan for the world if we had been subjected to the lights of publicity during those years. But, the world is more sophisticated and prepared to march towards a world government. The supernational sovereignty of an intellectual elite and world bankers is surely preferable to the national auto-determination practiced in past centuries."[14]

Many Americans have observed that the major media in the United States resembles a state- or party-run entity more than a free press. With such massive power, it has not only been able to suppress critical information from reaching its readers and viewers but has also possessed the power to alter long-held beliefs. Especially those relating to faith.

For the Beast Kingdom to rise, Christian teachings had to be diminished and replaced with secular humanism. Wherein man puts himself at the top instead of God. The foundation of Satanism. And this secret ruling cabal, with their unlimited financial wealth, began using it to take control of the new mass communication technology of television. Enabling it to minister into the homes of almost every citizen a new dark spiritual belief system. At first, subtly redirecting beliefs away from the Lord. Then much more openly. A dark ministry enabled by technology. As television was being used in this way, the United Nations, representing "all nations," began doing its part.

The United Nations

Associated with the United Nations are organizations that are called non-government organizations. Or "NGOs". And once recognized by the U.N., they become a branch of it. One such NGO called Lucis Trust would be used to redirect nations toward this "new world order." Formerly known as Lucifer Publishing, this offshoot of the United Nations was the brainchild of Alice Bailey. A dedicated occultist communicating with a Tibetan spirit that called itself Djwahl Kuhl. Guided by that spirit, she would go on to write twenty-eight occultist books, one of which was *The Externalization of the Hierarchy*.[15]

In that book, the Luciferian writer references "points of light" as a group of world leaders who serve the "Forces of Light." Satan presents himself as a spirit of light, enabling him to deceive the unsaved. Such a strange "points of light" statement would not be expected to be repeated by others. Unless they were sending a message. Yet, it was used by someone at the top of the political order. In his inaugural address on January 20, 1989, President George H.W. Bush spoke of "a thousand points of light." He was referencing "community organizations." Perhaps using that particular phrase was only a coincidence. But one would think the standard procedure before naming a presidential program would be to research names. And if it had been researched, they would have easily found that the phrase was associated with Satanism.

Many people involved in the creation of the United Nations had good vision and goals for the organization. First among them was the prevention of another world war. However, centralized power begs for dark forces to move in. And by the time Robert Mueller became Assistant Secretary General, the world body of "all nations" would take an even deeper step into darkness. With the power of the U.N. behind him, he would implement Bailey's writings to fundamentally change the way children are taught in public schools across the world. Bailey's dark goals listed in her book stated the need to fundamentally change religious values, primarily by taking God out of the education system. One method was to teach children in a way that broke the bond of parental authority over them. Not coincidentally, a break with the commandment to honor one's mother and father found in 2 Timothy 3:1-5. "This know also, that in the last days perilous times shall come. For men shall be lovers of their own selves, covetous, boasters, proud, blasphemers, disobedient to parents, unthankful, unholy."

These writings guiding the U.N.'s "educational" push were spelled out clearly by Bailey. As the decades since it was written would prove. About the family unit, she would write: "It is oppressive and that the family is the core of the nation. If you break the family, you break the nation. Liberate the people from the confines of this structure."[16] She also spoke about free sex without obligation or commitment. Saying, "Build clinics for abortion – Health clinics in schools. If people are going to enjoy the joy of sexual relationships, they need to be free of unnecessary fears, in other words, they should not be hampered with unwanted pregnancies."[17] Yet abortion is murder, and free sex is fornication, according to the Lord. Divorce and homosexuality were also encouraged by Bailey in her book. In it, like a dark prophetess, she foretold the use of mass media to promote all of these mindset changes. She also took a direct stab at Christianity itself.

Satan does not waste the time of his unwitting workers in this world by having them attack false religions. He promotes them. Bailey — working the will of her dark master— would go on to write about the need to "Promote other faiths to be at par with Christianity, and break this thing about Christianity as being the only way to heaven, by that Christianity will be pulled down and other faiths promoted...The church must change its doctrine and accommodate the people by accepting these things and putting them into its structure and systems."[18] This, too would unfold as decades passed.

That the United Nations — a one-world government project in itself — would indirectly embrace such teachings reflects the dark nature that overtook it. Its success in implementing these changes within the United States and Europe is most notable. Educators within the U.S. have guided this project into school systems across the land. Urging the implementation of Bailey's concepts was the *Humanist Manifesto,* introduced in 1933. One of its co-signers, C.F. Potter, prophetically wrote:

> "Education is thus a most powerful ally of humanism, and every American public school is a school of humanism. What can the theistic Sunday schools, meeting for an hour once a week, teach only a fraction of the children, do to stem the tide of a five-day program of humanistic teaching?"[19]

Satan's New World Order is the Beast Kingdom

The forces behind these attacks against Christianity have been unstoppable for several decades. The ultra-powerful force pushing it has remained hidden behind a curtain of darkness, working the wicked will of its true master, Satan. Parlaying its great success in the year 1913 to financially corrupt a multitude of institutions and major corporations. With such takeovers, this dark force has driven a dagger into the underpinnings of Christian civilization in Western Europe and America. And in so doing, it is fulfilling Biblical prophecy leading up to the launch of the end times. In political circles, this entity is given the name "New World Order. And for good reason. It is driving the world toward a dark order of spiritual beliefs and total economic and financial control, and it is also a name that has been used by a multitude of powerful people, including certain leaders, over time. But in the Bible, this entity is given a different name. The Beast Kingdom. The kingdom that the Antichrist will one day rule with a brutal rod.

The Beast Kingdom

The prophet Daniel said that the Beast Kingdom "shall be diverse from all kingdoms before it." Being "diverse" or different from all other kingdoms before it means we are not to look for the typical type of kingdom when identifying it. But rather a kind of kingdom that the world has never before seen. And that brings us back to the entity called the New World Order. Which is, undoubtedly, the entity Wilson and others wrote about. This hidden entity is proving itself to be the most powerful kingdom ever. Yet it has no borders. And this is new and "diverse" or "different." It is opposed to borders and directs its puppet leaders as such. Although it has no military, it possesses many militaries. Being able to direct the armies of nations led by leaders it places in power or who are surrounded by its minions. As mentioned earlier, this likely explains the paradox of the rider of the "white horse" of Revelation 6. He conquers with a "bow," but he has no arrows.

> [2]And I saw, and behold a white horse: and he that sat on him had a bow; and a crown was given unto him: and he went forth conquering, and to conquer.
> Revelation 6

The rider of the "white horse" is the Antichrist. He is conquering the world with only a "bow." He has no arrows. Now this makes sense. Because the New World Order/Beast Kingdom does not have its own army. It is a borderless kingdom that uses the armies of the nations whose rulers it controls. Directing the militaries of nations to do the conquering. Their arrows do the destroying launched by his order—his "bow." Which is essentially what the New World Order is currently doing. Even today, Americans see the U.S. and other Western governments using their militaries in ways that not only do not promote the safety of their own nations but destabilize the world. It is as though someone behind the scenes is now directing Western military actions. A hidden, dark entity. A "diverse" or "different" borderless kingdom — the New World Order. The Beast Kingdom.

We do not know who the current leader of the New World Order/ Beast Kingdom is. Or how many leaders it has already had. Because the entity written about by Wilson, Quigley, and a host of others lurks in the shadows. A place Quigley says it wants to stay. And if Quigley knew who its leaders were when he studied it in the 1960s, he was not telling. Nor did Wilson mention a single name. The creature wants to remain in the shadows. Controlling a host of nations from the dark place of a hidden kingdom. Based on the great success it has enjoyed over the last hundred years in promoting a one-world government and destroying Christian virtue, we can make a certain general assumption about its age. Which is very useful in determining how close the Antichrist is to taking the throne. And he should be very close!

If it is true that the Beast Kingdom assumed its Biblically foretold ruling structure several decades ago, then the New World Order/Beast Kingdom has evolved to the point wherein it has already had a series of leaders. And that is highly significant. Because the Antichrist will be its "sixth king," according to the scriptural case to be presented. It will also be presented that, along with a series of leaders, it also has a ruling council of ten. A group whose responsibilities include choosing its kings. With all ten ultimately becoming kings, each with a literal kingdom to rule. These are the ten kingdoms foretold by the prophets that will be associated with the Antichrist. And, finally, the case will be presented that events in recent years indicate a new level of deception and "dark sentences" has arrived. Being employed against the entire world, indicating the Antichrist is now actively engaged. Another reason he should be very near the throne now.

DAVID BRENNAN, SR.

A Paradox

Considering all of the dark goals achieved by the New World Order, if that entity is not the prophetically foretold Beast Kingdom, then it creates a strange paradox. Since over the course of time the New World Order has successfully checked off so many of the boxes indicated in Scripture that the Biblical Beast Kingdom will fulfill, if it is not the foretold Beast Kingdom, but just another satanic confederacy of men, then the Beast Kingdom will actually have competition when it arrives. This would also mean that Satan has his house divided. And that should be a bridge too far to cross for anyone who respects the prophets. The New World Order is a dark and massively powerful borderless kingdom, "diverse" or "different" from all kingdoms before it. Just as Daniel indicated the Beast Kingdom would be.

30

Chapter Three

THE BEAST KINGDOM: HIDDEN IN PLAIN SIGHT

A great storm is beginning to batter the world. Its winds even now steadily grow in intensity with the passing of each year. Like an unsuspecting island deep in outer space, the earth is beginning to convulse from the first outer tentacles of the twisting menace. Not aware that these initial outer bands pale in comparison to what is coming. Years the Biblical locusts have waited for.

As a child growing up in New Orleans, it was common to hear grownups talking about "the big one." The killer hurricane that would devastate the city. But it never came. Until it finally did. That horror was named Katrina. And the warnings of the church in America and elsewhere seem to have been playing out in a similar fashion. All the warnings that the end times were about to lurch upon the world have gone unfulfilled. Until they are fulfilled.

Some like to compare the moral degeneration in America and the West to that of certain ancient kingdoms. And certainly, both have much in common. But there is one big difference. None of those ancient nations had Christ as the focal point of their faith. At one time, America and the West did. Christianity overcame the powerful Roman Empire one believer at a time. Ultimately, conquering both Europe and America. Then America and the West moved away from Christ. Even after tasting His goodness. Psalm 9:17 gives a sobering reminder of the fate that awaits nations that forget God. In it, we are told: "The wicked shall be turned into hell, and all the nations that forget God." Yet, at the same time, Christians in America sent missionaries across the globe in obedience to the great commission. Shall that be the saving grace for America from a just and holy God?

The signs that the Beast Kingdom foretold by the prophets has been developing have been in plain sight before the church for decades. One sign is that although the United States is still technically considered a republic, wherein the people elect their representatives, the reality is that government by and for the people ended some time ago. And in its place has evolved a kind of satanic theocracy dedicated to promoting the will of Satan instead of the will of God. A sign that the Beast Kingdom was on the world stage. This sad transition from Christian freedom to a form of dark dictatorship has crept upon the nation in steps. Causing the proverbial frog to not notice the water getting hotter. A nation felled by mass media controlled by a small cabal of satanic ministers clothed as journalists. In league with Hollywood hedonists, producing programming designed to purge the last vestiges of Christian virtue from the culture.

A nation whose power centers were infiltrated by legions of Nazis after World War Two. Like the Biblical wolves clothed as sheep, they have altered American centers of power. From a nation of God-fearing people to a nation that follows the lust of the flesh and eyes and the pride of life. And the transition now appears complete. Producing individuals primed to be good citizens of the Beast Kingdom. A transition indicating an extraordinarily evil entity has gained power. A sign of an organized effort and not happenstance. A sign of a new kind of kingdom at work.

Romans 1 speaks to such a "reprobate mind" as what now rules America. Where sin is celebrated instead of hidden. Much as it was in the ancient cities of Sodom and Gomorrah. We are told in Daniel 11:37 that the Antichrist will not seek the affection of women. In line with that characteristic, legions of men have been led away from "the natural use of the woman, burned in their lust one toward another; men with men working that which is unseemly, and receiving in themselves that recompence of their error which was meet." But the transition from a God-centered culture to one ready to receive the Antichrist — carefully crafted and molded over decades — has many other dark attributes associated with it. Fulfilling the warnings found in Romans 1, the preparation of the Western nations to follow the Antichrist now appears to be complete. But God always has a remnant.

Opposition to the God of the Bible has been the main thrust of a steady drumbeat of media programming cloaked as entertainment. Especially directed toward turning the young away from God and toward a twisted version of compassion that accepts all aberrant behavior. The examples of this cultural shift are as numerous and deep as the culture itself. Such darkness as a child transitioning from male or female into something else. As though something else existed. As well as the slaughter of babies by the millions. A sacrifice to the demon god Moloch that was thought to have ended long ago. Such horrific practices indicate the evolution of the Beast Kingdom right before our eyes. And embracing such sin brings a nation to the point of insanity. A condition now visibly evident.

The media barrage of godless programming and indoctrination has unfolded along the lines of media consolidation. The more concentrated the media has become, the darker it has grown. Indicating a common force at work in this gathering of media power into the hands of the few. With the creation of the Federal Reserve decades ago, which placed massive financial resources in the hands of a few, it supplied unlimited funding for the takeover of the massive media complex in America and the western world. Whereas in America in 1983 there were 50 dominant media corporations, today there are five, controlling about 90 percent of media in the United States.[1] And this concentration has not only empowered the indoctrination of dark anti-Christian beliefs but has also been used to oppress political forces opposed to their implementation.

Evidencing centralized control and coordination of actions. Further indicating the dark tentacles of the same godless creature. The Beast Kingdom.

Concentrated control of major media and the production facilities of Hollywood has been used toward programming designed to alter long-held Christian beliefs related to sexuality. Taking America from a nation where adultery and sex out of wedlock were looked down upon. To a nation that celebrates all forms of sexual activity outside marriage. Including lesbianism and homosexuality. The methodical effort to turn the nation's culture onto this dark pathway is the obvious result of a concerted effort. And such an effort demands an organized entity behind it. The Beast Kingdom.

Former great institutions of learning — founded on Christ-based principles — have experienced their own transition. From centers of higher education to centers of indoctrination in anti-Christian theology. With numbers upwards of 88% of college professors indicating a "liberal" ideological embrace and only 9% embracing traditional beliefs.[2] Demonstrating a purging of educators whose time-tested beliefs are apparently the reason they do not get hired. Effectively transitioning former institutions of higher education into indoctrination centers. Not only priming young minds to become purveyors of an anti-Christian theology, but also turning many into politically intolerant individuals willing to actively suppress the liberties and speech of those who express Christian beliefs. If that sounds familiar, it should. It is another characteristic of those who serve the Beast Kingdom.

The transition process for students has also included a move from patriotism to internationalism. Another Beast Kingdom goal. All evolving right before the eyes of the church in a way that speaks to an organized entity engaged in warfare against it. All of this has been another sign that the Beast Kingdom is busy at work within the world. But it is not limited there. The attacks have come against key government institutions as well.

Federal Law Enforcement Agencies:
Brazenly Open Corruption

Recent years have shown that the corruption of federal law enforcement agencies within the United States now appears complete. It has become apparent that if a political figure promotes the will of the Beast Kingdom (abortion, homosexuality, lesbianism, transgenderism, socialism, etc.), they are virtually immune from federal investigation and prosecution. But those considered a threat could suddenly die in prison. Political figures fighting the Beast Kingdom receive a different standard. The case of Donald Trump comes to mind.

Trump had both the Federal Bureau of Investigation (FBI) and the Department of Justice (DOJ) take actions against him that can best be described as a "witch hunt."[3] A term more appropriate than many realize, considering the kingdom ultimately behind the attacks. Both federal agencies were willing to suffer damaged reputations to take him down. Falsifying "evidence," raiding his home — a first in presidential history — colluding with major media outlets to spread "fake news" stories — government censorship of information — a direct challenge to the U.S. Constitution— to name a few.[4] Although apparently limited to their upper ranks, the damage done by these corrupt actors left the reputations of both institutions in tatters. The good agents soiled with the bad. Yet the upper ranks did it anyway. No doubt, the authoritarian indoctrination from the universities their leadership likely experienced coming into play. Indicating a form of immoral control at work behind the scenes. Another sign.

In line with its evolving anti-Christian thrust, the FBI would raid the family home of a pro-life Christian activist in the early morning hours. The other option for his arrest was to simply knock on his door in the middle of the day, since he posed no threat.[5] But a point was being made. One to instill terror. Oppose the anti-God agenda of such things as abortion, and your door could get kicked in during the middle of the night. An approach the ancient demon god Moloch would have approved of. Following through on this approach, the DOJ threatened Christian activists with 11 years in jail for opposing abortion.[6] However, such FBI and DOJ intimidation is no longer limited to Christian activists. But anyone who stands against the political and spiritual goals of the New World Order/Beast Kingdom. This includes their own people.

An FBI whistleblower exposing the "persecutions" of conservatives and Christians within the FBI would find out the hard way. Being suspended from the FBI and stripped of his badge and gun. His offense? Exposing the anti-Christian drive that has taken over the FBI.[7] And the Democratic Party, compromised over decades into becoming a tentacle of the New World Order/Beast Kingdom, pleased by the new direction of both the FBI and DOJ, would seek a dramatic increase in funding to fight "extremist violence and domestic terrorists."[8] Catchwords for Christians and conservatives. Such dark actions likely enabled due to their university experiences. Ready to answer the call of political oppression. All of this is another sign there is a new force in control of the nation. One seeking authoritarian control. The Beast Kingdom.

On the international scene, there is an unholy alliance of Western nations that punishes those who follow the true God and promotes those who oppose Him. Institutions of health, education, finance, diplomacy, the media, major corporations, and a host of others now appear to obey directives that can only be described as dark or insane. This fits well with what Scripture tells us the ungodly Beast Kingdom will embrace. And embracing such godlessness causes the insanity now so prevalent. In the U.S. government financial aid to poor countries is now in many ways dependent on those nations promoting darkness in their cultures. On the international scene, there is something else happening. Perhaps for the first time in history.

Ending the Nation-State

Something new under the sun has happened. Leaders within many nations have been demoting national sovereignty in favor of another higher political power. And this is new. Within the nations doing this, their political class appears to be unwilling or unable to resist the drive. A drive coming from outside their nations. No doubt, from the entity Wilson wrote about. And those who resist are swiftly dealt with. A glaring example of this is the reaction of elite powers to the election of President Donald Trump. The entire thrust of his election centered on placing America first. As a result, the ruling elite set out to destroy him. And succeeded. The trend is unmistakable. This, too, is perfectly in line with an organized entity taking increasing control over the affairs of nations. A dark, hidden kingdom. Another clue that the Beast Kingdom has been evolving.

As all of these developments have unfolded — and much more — technological advancements have accelerated at a dizzying pace, placing power in the hands of morally degenerate people in a way never before imagined. The transition America has experienced has also happened in Western Europe. And it is America that has been the key to taking down the entire West through godless Hollywood exports. Effectively, exporting Satan to the rest of the world. It is the Western nations that are the most powerful, both economically and militarily. Essentially, the western bloc of nations has suffered the worst kind of defeat without firing a single shot. Felled from within. But behind all of this, there is a much greater meaning.

Beast Kingdom in Bible Prophecy

If the New World Order is the Beast Kingdom, then it must be in line with Bible prophecy and not conflict with it. Bible prophecy cannot be wrong because it was given by God to His prophets. There have been examples in the recent past when Christians suspected they had found the Beast Kingdom. Only to later be proven wrong. One example was during the tumultuous 1930s and 1940s. As Christians watched the Nazi Third Reich — making war and persecuting the Jews — many believed it might be the Beast Kingdom. However, although Adolf Hitler was clearly a type of antichrist, he was not the Antichrist, nor was Germany the Beast Kingdom. But a prototype of it.

One scriptural method of understanding that the Nazis could not be the Beast Kingdom was the fact that the State of Israel was not back in the land yet. And their return to the land was an absolute necessity for end time prophecy to unfold according to the prophets. Those who thought Germany was the Beast Kingdom were sincere but off the mark. They were off the mark because they did not take the prophecy Scriptures literally enough when they were told Israel would return as a nation by such prophecies as the Valley of Dry Bones found in Ezekiel 37. And for the New World Order to be the Beast Kingdom, it, too, must not conflict with Bible prophecy.

Regarding the Scriptures, some would say there is one big scriptural perspective that stands in the way of the New World Order being the foretold Beast Kingdom. That teaching states that the Antichrist will arise out of a ten-kingdom confederacy of some kind. This teaching is based on Daniel 7, wherein we are told the Antichrist will arise "after" ten kings. And if that perspective is accurate, then since there is currently no such ten-kingdom entity, the New World Order cannot be the Beast Kingdom. And the end times are still far off. As mentioned previously, this author embraced that teaching for many years. However, it is this teaching that is at the center of the church missing the rise of the Beast Kingdom.

Ten Kingdoms

The Sixth King will not dispute that there is a ten-kingdom confederacy associated with the Beast Kingdom during the end times. That is a solid and indisputable prophetic truth. Multiple Scriptures relay this to us. However, although *The Sixth King* does not dispute that there is a ten-kingdom confederacy, it will hotly dispute the timing of its coming into being. What will be presented in the next chapter is that this evil confederacy is not in existence at the time the Antichrist rises to the beast throne. But springs up AFTER he becomes its king. It will be presented that a literal reading of Isaiah, Daniel, and Revelation offers no other conclusion when read in context. The same literal kind of reading that Christians should have employed in the past relative to the return of the nation of Israel.

From this prophetic perspective, the Beast Kingdom initially exists as a single entity, only later adding the ten kingdoms. With the lands for those ten new kingdoms coming about as a result of the Antichrist going about "conquering and to conquer" according to the first seal in Revelation 6. And this scriptural conclusion opens the door wide to the New World Order being the prophetically awaited Beast Kingdom. With the world on the brink of a time of trouble unlike any in its history.

Following that the "The Sixth King" chapter will present the case that this initial Beast Kingdom has a series of kings leading up to the Antichrist. Kingdoms typically have a series of kings. And the case will further be made that the Antichrist will be the sixth king in that lineage. This is also according to a literal reading of various Scriptures, as will be presented.

If this is true, then the succession of Beast Kingdom kings must be getting very close to the sixth king — the Antichrist — coming to power. In fact, in a later chapter, the case will also be made that the political, medical, and media events surrounding the COVID-19 pandemic demonstrate a level of deception that is a game changer. Representing the implementation of "dark sentences" on a level indicating the Antichrist is almost certainly on the scene and already influencing events. But first things first. The scriptural case that the ten kingdoms associated with the Beast Kingdom come into being only after the Antichrist rises to power. And that all ten kings initially come out of the Beast Kingdom while it is still a single massively powerful borderless kingdom.

Chapter Four

THE TEN KINGS: A RULING COUNCIL INITIALLY?

And I stood upon the sand of the sea, and saw a beast rise up out of the sea, having seven heads and ten horns, and upon his horns ten crowns, and upon his heads the name of blasphemy.

And the beast which I saw was like unto a leopard, and his feet were as the feet of a bear, and his mouth as the mouth of a lion: and the dragon gave him his power, and his seat, and great authority. Revelation 13:1-2

If the Beast Kingdom is the entity by the modern name of the New World Order, then its rise has been missed. And the likely reason for this grand oversight is the teaching that the Antichrist arises out of a ten-kingdom confederacy. This teaching has caused students of Bible prophecy to search for the signs of such a ten-nation/kingdom confederacy so the clock marking his rise can begin ticking. The fact there is a ten-kingdom confederacy associated with the Antichrist is an absolute scriptural truth. It will exist according to Daniel and John in Revelation. This chapter presents the scriptural case that the ten kingdoms arise only AFTER the Antichrist rises to the Beast Kingdom throne. Meaning there is nothing at present preventing his rise. In fact, later the case will be made that he is already acting in the world.

As a result of the belief that the ten kingdoms must first exist before the Antichrist can arise, that perspective has caused much attention to be focused on the European Union. A political and economic union of twenty-seven countries. And with European nations heavily under the influence of American cultural exports, primarily from Hollywood, many of the member nations have seen their cultures change dramatically in the sin-filled direction of the Beast Kingdom. However, the obvious problem with the European Union somehow evolving into a ten-kingdom beast confederacy is its size. There are twenty-seven, not ten. Nor does it appear that seventeen members will be leaving the union any time soon.

One of the first problems in identifying the Beast Kingdom is the description of it given by the prophets Daniel and John the Revelator. The verses at the beginning of this chapter depict a strange and mysterious entity. A Beast that will have seven heads, ten horns, and the appearance of a lion, leopard, and bear. But when breaking down each element, this strange entity starts taking a known shape.

The Ten Kings

The bazaar beast from the sea, rising up with seven heads and ten horns, is contorted with the images of a lion, leopard, and a bear. It is a foul thing filled with blasphemies that will take the lives and souls of countless millions. Consider the Scriptures speaking to the ten horns. And as with everything associated with the beast, the description of the ten horns is both strange and contradictory. We start with John's description found in Revelation 17.

> [12] "The ten horns which you saw are ten kings who have received <u>no kingdom as yet</u>, but they receive authority

for one hour as kings with the beast. [13] These are of one mind, and they will give their power and authority to the beast. Revelation 17

They are "kings." But they have "no kingdom." "Yet." But they are "kings." How can they be called "kings" before they receive their "kingdom?" The answer given in the verses is that they "receive authority for one hour as kings with the beast." These are instant, "one hour" kingships, but without actual kingdoms. Essentially, they are "kings" on paper only at this point. Why would the Antichrist award such fleeting "one hour" kingships to them? Because he wants each to have the title of king. Why is that so important? Because it means that when, as "kings," they give their "power and authority" to him, then he can claim to be a "king of kings." Mimicking Jesus' title as the real "King of kings." This is why, after receiving authority for "one hour as kings"—not a "kingdom" for "one hour," but only "authority for one hour as kings"—and being of "one mind," they return their momentary power to the beast. It is all done to blaspheme Christ.

To gain additional context on these odd kings, there is a little-noticed Scripture found in the Book of Isaiah. In it, the prophet repeats words that the Antichrist will one day say. On their own, these words make little sense. Until they are put in context with Revelation 17, where they are referred to as "kings" when they do not "yet" have an actual kingdom. Isaiah appears to be telling us what stations they possess at the time the Antichrist grants them their title of kings.

[8]For <u>he</u> says, 'Are not my <u>princes</u> altogether <u>kings</u>?
Isaiah 10:8

The Hebrew word for "princes" is the masculine noun "sar," used to identify various types of leaders. In the Old Testament, it is used 208 times for prince, 130 times for captain, 33 times for chief, and 33 times for ruler. So these could be literal princes or simply notable leaders. Another key in the verse is "he." It is the Antichrist. Seven verses earlier, "he" references "O Assyrian rod of My anger." The Lord's anger. And we know from Micah 5:1-6 that the "Assyrian" is the Antichrist because at the beginning of those verses, "Bethlehem, Ephratah," is identified as where "this man" Jesus will be born. Then this is in verse 5:

> ...⁵And this man shall be the peace, when the Assyrian shall come into our land: and when he shall tread in our palaces, then shall we raise against him seven shepherds, and eight principal men. Micah 5:5

This action of the "Assyrian" has never taken place. It has yet to happen. And when it does happen, it will be Jesus who deals with him. This is an end time event, with the Antichrist simply being called by one of his many names found throughout Scripture. There is also Isaiah 31:4–9. Within those verses, the "Assyrian" is being dealt with by Jesus when the Lord comes back in the second coming. "Then the Assyrian shall fall by a sword, not of man, and a sword not of mankind shall devour him." Isaiah chapters 14 and 10 also speak of the Assyrian as the Antichrist.

These "princes" that the Antichrist indicates are his "kings" must also be the same "ten kings" described in Revelation 17. That is because these ten kings are the only kings that Scripture tells us are intimately associated with him. This would explain why Revelation 17 describes the ten kings as those "who have received no kingdom as yet." They must first be "princes" or powerful leaders who later receive their kingdoms to rule. That is why these ten princes or leaders must be granted "authority for one hour as kings." When later they receive their actual kingdoms, then they become real "kings." And there may be something else going on here with these "kings."

Since these "one hour" "kings" are destined to each receive actual kingdoms, it may also be the case that John is simply using the title of what they ultimately become. "Kings" with actual kingdoms. And not by the lesser position they will hold along the way. "Princes." Consider the example of former President Franklin D. Roosevelt, which is informative to this point.

Before he became President of the United States, he was first Governor of New York. But historically, no one refers to him as Governor Roosevelt. He is always referred to by the ultimate office he attained. President Roosevelt. That is because we are looking from the present back in time, so we refer to him by the ultimate title he attained. However, the truth is that he was governor of a major state before he attained this lofty position. And it was his stepping stone to the presidency. It could truthfully be said by New Yorkers of Roosevelt: "Is not my governor also a president?" And if a prophet had foretold his rise, would he not have referred to Roosevelt as a president even though he was a governor first?

Either John is describing them as "kings" because they will ultimately be real "kings," and he is looking backwards at the reality of what they ultimately become, or it is because they are made "kings" for "one hour," essentially granting them the title of king on paper only at that point. But he cannot be referring to them as "kings" because they have kingdoms at the time they lift the Antichrist to the throne. Because Revelation 17 makes it clear they do not "yet" have an actual kingdom then. It should also be noted that because they have to be made "kings" for "one hour," that they do not even have the title of king until that hour. As well as no actual kingdom! This, too, speaks to the reality of their lower station as "princes" or notable leaders initially.

Daniel and the Antichrist

The prophet Daniel also speaks about these "ten kings." And some of what he says is used by those who believe the Antichrist must arise from within a ten-kingdom confederacy. But that perspective is challenged by a certain part of Daniel's words as well as the direct statements of Revelation 17 as well as Isaiah 10. The prophet starts by setting the stage.

> [23]Thus he said, The fourth beast shall be the fourth kingdom upon earth, which shall be diverse from all kingdoms, and shall devour the whole earth, and shall tread it down, and break it in pieces. Daniel 7:23

Of all the kingdoms that have existed on the earth, the beast kingdom will be "diverse" ("different" NKJV) from them. And this direct statement of Scriptural truth from Daniel opens the door to a new kind of kingdom — one that has never before existed. The borderless New World Order. Not only will the beast kingdom "be diverse from all kingdoms" that have ever existed on the earth, but it will "devour the whole earth." The ancient words say it will be the whole earth. And thus the need for his ten princes to oversee a vast expanse of conquered lands, making them actual kings. Now Daniel's words concerning the "ten kings" and the Antichrist.

> [24]And the ten horns out of this kingdom are ten kings that shall arise: and **another** shall rise after them; and **he** shall be diverse from the first, and he shall subdue three kings. Daniel 7:24

Because this Scripture states that the Antichrist ("another") "shall rise after them," many assume that these wicked kings will have their kingdoms at the time when the Antichrist rises to the Beast Kingdom throne. And this is not an unreasonable perspective. Because it embraces a direct statement of Scripture. The truth is they are "kings" at the time the Antichrist "shall rise after them." Because according to Revelation 17, they are "one hour" "kings." And this allows the Antichrist to rise to the throne "after them" when they have the title of "kings" (on paper) so he can mimic Christ as a king of kings. This perspective conforms to Revelation 17, which tells us the "ten kings" have no kingdoms "yet." It also conforms to the fact that they are "kings." While at the same time acknowledging that the Antichrist will "rise after them."

Within the first half of the verse is a statement that also supports these perspectives. We are told that "the ten horns out of this kingdom are ten kings that shall arise." We are being told that these ten kings arise out of a single kingdom! "Out of this kingdom." Singular. And obviously, there cannot be ten kings simultaneously ruling a single kingdom. This odd statement can only make sense in the context that they initially hold a lesser position within a single kingdom — the Beast Kingdom — as princes or significant leaders, also being made "kings" on paper only. All of which is until they receive actual kingdoms fulfilling the "yet" in Revelation 17.

Since we are also told the Antichrist "shall rise after them," we can understand that these princes or leaders have been established within this unusual and different Beast Kingdom before the ascension of the Antichrist within it. And if they are "princes" or leaders of some kind within the New World Order/Beast Kingdom, then we can speculate that they must be some kind of council of ten that are present in their ruling positions at the time the Antichrist rises above them to power. All within the initial single Beast Kingdom before it adds the ten kingdoms.

The Power Play

It is clear that as the Antichrist strives for the throne of this different beast kingdom, he will not initially have the support of all ten. We are told he has to subdue three of them. But it is equally apparent that after doing so, those three return to his good graces. We know this because we are told in Revelation 17 that all ten are destined to possess literal kingdoms. Revelation 17 also tells us all ten "have one mind, and shall give their power and strength unto the beast." As well as all ten being made "kings" for "one hour."

This power play, wherein the Antichrist overcomes and then restores three kings, appears to be a reflection of some kind of internal political intrigue within the Beast Kingdom. And it is ripe for speculation. Relating to the three he overcomes, the Hebrew verb "shephal" is used for subdue, and it essentially means to humble. Earlier in Daniel 7, we are told of those three: "They were plucked up by the roots." Indicating a much rougher handling of them will initially take place before they come to their dark senses and support the Antichrist.

The restoration of the three princes or leaders whom he will pluck out or humble may be related to his needing to placate some of the ten. Remember, Daniel 7 tells us that not only will the Beast Kingdom be "diverse" or "different" from all kingdoms before it, but that the Antichrist himself will also be "diverse" or "different" from the ten. It would appear that part of this difference is that the ten have longevity greater than his own within the Beast Kingdom, since we are told Antichrist "shall rise after them." Or it could be that all ten have such strong power bases within the beast kingdom that he has no choice. It is likely that the restoration of those three whom the Antichrist subdues will be born out of some kind of practical political necessity.

Whether or not the ten are aware that the future holds actual kingdoms for them, we cannot know. But it is likely that as the Antichrist ascends to the throne of the Beast Kingdom, he has already developed his plan to conquer the world. (Covered in the chapter titled "Trojan Horses") So what better carrot to dangle before the ten than the promise of actual kingdoms in the future? Not just the title of king accompanied by an hour of "authority." But where does the territory come from for these ten princes to receive kingdoms?

Ten Kingdom Territories

That answer appears to be found in Revelation 6. It is there that we see the Antichrist riding the "white horse" of the Apocalypse, going about "conquering and to conquer." And as the verse states, he only has a "bow" but no arrows. As mentioned earlier that is because the Beast Kingdom is "diverse" or "different" from all kingdoms before it, just as Daniel said it would be. It is the most powerful kingdom in world history. A borderless kingdom that takes down nations from within, ruling from the shadows through leaders loyal to it. Leaders put in office by its minions who are dedicated to its dark agenda or who are power hungry. Directing the militaries of those nations according to its unholy will. Even stealing elections. So when the great war launching the end times begins, the Antichrist has clean hands in the sight of the world since he will not send any arrows directly. That is why he is riding a "white horse." It is the perfect deception, causing legions of the unwitting to follow him when he brings "peace." Brilliant!

And those conquered countries will need rulers loyal to him. What better group than his ten princes to fulfill Isaiah's statement: "For he says, 'Are not my princes altogether kings?'" Yes, they will become kings because the Antichrist is the one who makes them so because they are his "princes." But only after he rises to power within the strange beast kingdom and begins conquering.

A Ruling Council?

The prophet Isaiah refers to the "ten kings" as "princes" when he informs us as to how the Antichrist will view them before they become actual kings with a kingdom. But as previously mentioned, the Hebrew masculine noun "sar" is used for "princes" in the verse. Which not only means a literal royal "prince," but also simply a significant leader.

Additionally, we find that as powerful as the Antichrist is, it appears he must deal with these ten with great care, indicating they have significant power within the ruling structure of the Beast Kingdom while it exists as a single entity. How do we know this?

Because even though Daniel 7:24 informs us that the Antichrist "shall subdue three kings" in his rise above them, we learn from Revelation 17 that ultimately all ten become actual kings with a kingdom. Apparently, doing otherwise would be a major political headache for him. The only logical reason for his having to deal with them with such caution is that they are an important part of the Beast Kingdom even before becoming actual kings. They are so important that after the Antichrist gains enormous tracks of lands across the globe, as he goes about "conquering and to conquer" in Revelation 6, it is these ten leaders that he appoints as "kings" to rule over them. This appears to be a practical political payoff. And that the Antichrist has to overcome three also shows they have real power. We know the ten have a power base because Revelation 17 makes it clear they are deeply involved in the process of choosing beast kings.

The most logical conclusion from all this is that these ten "princes" or leaders must be some form of ruling council that chooses beast kings when the throne becomes open either through death or the completion of a term. Since we do not know the inner workings of it beyond what Scripture tells us, we do not know the details of how a beast kingship ends. It is a kingdom shrouded in darkness. The place Satan likes to dwell. But since they are referred to as "kings," it is likely their rule ends at death. Which is the typical way a king's rule ends. It also follows that the most likely source for picking Beast Kingdom kings would be from within this group of ten leaders. Why would they look elsewhere? They know each other and the inner workings of the Beast Kingdom. This likely explains why three do not initially support the Antichrist taking the throne. Perhaps one of them seeks the throne for himself. But seven are so impressed with the Antichrist that they bypass their group and support him.

Since we are dealing with a "different" kind of kingdom — one that works its darkness from the shadows just as all of Satan's empire does — then we cannot know for certain what role any of the major figures in today's news might play. We can only speculate as to this at present. But there should be at least 11 ultra-powerful people at the top. That being a "king" as well as a council of ten. All of which is perfectly in line with a ruling structure able to placate numerous powerful factions within the same kingdom at the same time. And there is a certain question that needs to be addressed. How can the Antichrist come "after" the "ten" and then rise above them to take the throne?

A Fierce Man Understanding Dark Sentences

Since these ten princes or leaders are in strong political positions within the Beast Kingdom before Antichrist's rise, he would need to possess an impressive set of persuasion skills to outwit and overcome them. Power politics demands this. We know from Scripture that he does just that in an amazing feat of political jousting skills.

Such skills would appear to relate to the beastly nature of the Antichrist as described by the prophets. Daniel chapter 8 describes him as having a "fierce countenance." Exactly what those features are, we are not told. However, we do know that, from the perspective of men, he is viewed as fierce. Typically, such fierceness instills fear. Daniel 7 sums up the impact of his appearance by simply saying, "whose look was more stout than his fellows." And this physical appearance is combined with an uncanny understanding of sinister schemes, making his ability to outmaneuver opponents unmatched. In fact, Scripture describes him as having an understanding of "dark sentences." Meaning he not only has an uncanny ability to understand the most difficult riddles and perplexing questions, but also dark and obscure utterances, leaving the ten princes-kings hopelessly outgunned as well as completely impressed.

This probably explains why only three oppose the usurper rising above them within this strangely "different" Beast Kingdom to ultimately rule it. As for the seven who do not oppose him, they are apparently so impressed with him that they set aside their own political ambitions in support and ultimately receive a large demonic payoff. Becoming actual kings over parts of the conquered lands. And those lands will be massive. But such demonic understanding and fierceness can come from only one source. Satan.

> [24]His power shall be mighty, but not by his own power.
> Daniel 8:24

Daniel goes on to describe how destructive he will be. But despite his destructiveness — or perhaps because of it — he "shall prosper and thrive." And in line with understanding difficult riddles and "dark sentences," he is "cunning" and "shall cause deceit to prosper under his rule." Through dark understandings derived supernaturally from Satan, he is the most treacherous leader to ever walk the earth. That says a lot considering the litany of monsters history has unleashed on unsuspecting generations. This is what these ten princes are up against, and they are no match.

Signs of the Antichrist's Presence

The rise of the Antichrist within the Beast Kingdom likely comes from his impressive set of skills. He is capable of coming up with plans so detailed, cunning, and effective in dark brilliance as to clearly show himself to be at a level well above the ten who have had status within the Beast Kingdom before his entry into its upper ranks. And based on the unfolding of an incredibly well-formulated dark plan in recent years — at a level never before witnessed in world history — this indicates there is now a force within the Beast Kingdom that has brought it to a level of deadly cunning and "dark sentences" beyond anything ever before seen in world history. And this is the clearest evidence yet that the Antichrist is now involved in shaping the affairs of the world. (This will be covered in detail in the chapter titled, "Dark Sentences: The Signs Antichrist is Now Engaging the World.)

The scriptural perspective presented here indicates that the Beast Kingdom has a powerful group of ten leaders who eventually become kings with actual kingdoms of their own. And that they are deeply involved in the process of choosing their kings. As such, as the next chapter will show, the Beast Kingdom has already had a number of kings for some time. Exactly how long we do not know. We cannot know what number king it is currently being ruled by. But based on certain historical factors, a general estimate of what number the Beast Kingdom is currently on can be made.

Being a completely different kind of kingdom, as noted by Daniel — a borderless kingdom usurping national sovereignty — plumbing its inner workings is not easy. However, as the next chapter shows, what we do know is that the Antichrist will be its sixth king. And that he should now be very close to the throne.

Chapter Five

THE SIXTH KING

Within the first verses of Revelation 13, there is a mysterious beast described in terms that are both strange and fearsome. It is a twisted and freakish entity better suited for the winding and fiery caverns of hell than the earth. It is a beast the like of which has never before been seen until it rises up from the sea of politics with the help of the dragon, its blasphemies going before it in a plague of sin and death across the entire earth. Understanding this dark creature is to understand the essence of the Antichrist and the Beast Kingdom. It is a kingdom that has three distinct parts: "Heads, horns", and animal-like features. And each of these characteristics symbolizes an element of this dark empire.

> [1]And I stood upon the sand of the sea, and saw a beast rise up out of the sea, having seven heads and ten horns, and upon his horns ten crowns, and upon his heads the name of blasphemy.
>
> [2] And the beast which I saw was like unto a leopard, and his feet were as the feet of a bear, and his mouth as the mouth of a lion: and the dragon gave him his power, and his seat, and great authority. Revelation 13

There are two groups of kings intimately associated with the Beast Kingdom. One group — the seven heads — informs us there is a succession of kings leading up to the Antichrist. This succession demonstrates both the preexisting nature of the Beast Kingdom at the time the Antichrist rises to its throne as well as exactly where within the succession he comes to power. His rise to the throne is through the ten horns, which other Scriptures tell us are ten kings who eventually will have actual kingdoms of their own. But not at the time when the Antichrist assumes the throne, according to Revelation 17.

The Sixth King

Certain prophecy Scriptures explain John's strange beast, and they are presented in the form of riddles. Each is a mystery. And this is done with purpose. Only the correct answer will resolve these mysterious verses. And the strange description of the "seven heads," which are both mountains as well as kings, appears to be understood by this approach. When the correct answer is found, it will fit within and not conflict with the other Scriptures associated with it. In this way, it is possible to know that the correct answer has been found in explaining the strange "seven heads" of the Beast Kingdom. Consider the following passage, which presents the beast (Antichrist) in the form of a riddle.

> [8]The beast that you saw was and is not, and will ascend out of the bottomless pit and go to perdition. And those who dwell on the earth will marvel, whose names are not written in the Book of Life from the foundation of the world, when they see the beast that was, and is not, and yet is. Revelation 17:8

The beast referred to is the Antichrist. How can the Antichrist be the "beast that was, and is not, and yet is"? We are literally being told he exists, then does not exist, and then does exist. By itself, this passage is a mystery dangling in the mind of man. It is part of the Antichrist puzzle. Now here is another passage relating to the "seven heads" that presents them as a succession of Beast Kingdom kings leading up to the Antichrist. It, too, presents a riddle to be resolved using another Scripture that will shortly be added.

> [9] "Here is the mind which has wisdom: The <u>seven heads</u> are seven mountains on which the woman sits. [10] There are also <u>seven kings</u>. Five have fallen, one is, and the other has not yet come. And when he comes, he must continue a short time. [11] <u>The beast that was, and is not, is himself also the eighth, and is of the seven</u>, and is going to perdition. Revelation 17:9-11

John tells us the "seven heads are seven mountains" as well as the "seven kings" on which the "woman sits." They support her. She is the Mother of Harlots, who is mentioned several verses earlier. About these "seven kings," we are told the following: "Five have fallen." Indicating the passing of "five" kings. "One is," which would be the sixth king, indicating he is the one to focus on. "And the other has not yet come. And when he comes, he must continue a short time." This would be the seventh king. This flow depicts a succession of beast kings covering the first five, then the sixth, and finally the seventh. Then we are given a mysterious passage wherein we are told the beast is "the eighth, and is of the seven." Here is the riddle. Although within this succession of rulers there are no more than "seven kings," and the beast (Antichrist) is one of the "seven," he is "also the eighth." How can he be the "eighth" when there are no more than "seven," of which he is one? It seems impossible.

The key to unlocking this passage and the flow of beast kings is found in Revelation 13. The chapter starts with the opening verses detailing a description of the Beast Kingdom by referencing the "seven heads," the ten horns, and the lion, leopard, and bear. After providing that description, John tells us about something happening to one of the "seven heads." When reading this verse, keep in mind that Revelation 17:9–11 defines the "seven heads" as a succession of seven kings. So when this Revelation 13 verse refers to a "head," it is referring back to one of those seven kings. The best interpreter of Scripture is Scripture itself.

> [3] And I saw one of his <u>heads</u> as if it had been mortally wounded, and his deadly wound was healed. And all the world marveled and followed the beast. Revelation 13:3

This Scripture directly tells us one of the "seven heads" suffers a "deadly wound," which then "was healed." We know from Revelation 17 what is meant by one of its "heads." We were told the "heads" represent a succession of kings leading up to the Antichrist. So we are very directly told that one of the kings within the succession of beast kings will suffer assassination. Then, shockingly, we are told he will come back to life again in a resurrection from the dead. In addition to the highly supernatural nature of this information, it allows us to now understand the previous verses describing the "seven heads" and how Antichrist can be the eighth even though there are no more than seven. And also that the Antichrist must be the sixth king in the succession of kings. Here is their resolution.

We know from Revelation 17:9–11 that the "seven heads" are not just "mountains," but also a succession of kings. We are told about the fate of the first five kings, then one that "is," another to come, and then the "eighth." So in Revelation 13, when we are told one of the "heads" suffers a "deadly wound," it is referring back to one of those "seven kings" suffering the "deadly wound." Because these "kings" are depicted as the "heads." But we are also told the "wound" will be "healed," and he will return from the dead in a kind of resurrection. This makes one of the "seven kings" the "beast that was, and is not, and yet is." Before suffering the "deadly wound," he "was," after the "deadly wound," he is not, and after it is healed, he "yet is." Since we are told the Antichrist is the "eighth king," he must also be the sixth king to solve the riddle. It must be the Antichrist — the sixth king — who suffers the "deadly wound." Then he is followed by the seventh king, who we are told lasts a "short time." And when the Antichrist comes back to life, he reassumes the throne as the "eighth king," displacing the seventh. We are told the seventh king lasts only a "short time" because the Antichrist does not stay dead for long. Possibly three days mimicking the resurrection of Christ. Even though there are only "seven kings," Antichrist is the "eighth" because he is both the sixth and the "eighth" king.

> (Some who read about the "beast" in Revelation 17 and in Revelation 13 and one of the "heads" being wounded to death see kingdoms of the past that disappeared and later came back. Instead of a man dying and coming back to life. However, the verses that follow in Revelation 13 seamlessly reference the beast as "him" and having a "mouth speaking great things," as well as "he opened his mouth in blasphemy," and "all that dwell upon the earth shall worship him," and so forth. All referencing a man and not kingdoms.)

As always you should check the Scriptures to see if you agree with these conclusions. Now consider the story in Daniel 11 about a vile king that relays the same sequence of events as just covered.

The Story of the Vile King

Daniel 11 starts by describing events involving kings in the distant past. Then, starting around verse 19, it transitions to events concerning the Antichrist. In it, a story is told of a "vile" leader. How bad is this man? Although the word "vile" is found 13 times in the Bible, this leader has the distinction of being the only person individually labeled as such by a prophet. And for good reason. He replaces a leader who held power for only a "few days." Oddly, the brief king relinquishes his crown in neither "anger or in battle." How unusual. Why would anyone strong enough to reach the throne give it up without a fight? By now, you should suspect that the Antichrist is involved. Because wherever he appears, so does a gnarled and perverse story that requires unraveling. And the process of unraveling this story takes us to the verse just before the brief leader appears. It describes the fate of the king just before him.

> [19]Then he shall turn his face toward the fortress of his own land; but he shall stumble and <u>fall</u>, and not be found. Daniel 11:19

This king shall "fall." The Hebrew verb for "fall" is "naphal," which occasionally means to "fall"—"of violent death," according to Strong's Concordance. A good example of this usage is found in Leviticus 26:7. "You will chase your enemies, and they shall <u>fall</u> by the sword before you." Now consider the leader that replaces him after his "fall."

> [20] There shall arise in his place one who imposes taxes on the glorious kingdom; but within <u>a few days</u> he shall be destroyed, but <u>not in anger or in battle</u>.

The key point is not that he "imposes taxes." But that "within a <u>few days</u> he shall be destroyed, but not in anger or in battle." He only remains in power for "a few days" and is not removed "in anger or in battle." Now consider the next person who takes over after the leader of a "few days" is gone.

> [21] And in his place shall arise a <u>vile person</u>, to whom they will not give the honor of royalty; but he shall come in peaceably, and seize the kingdom by intrigue. Daniel 11:20-21

It is generally accepted that the "vile person" is the Antichrist. And this conclusion becomes increasingly clear as his story continues until the end of Chapter 11. We are told he replaces the king, who only lasts a "few days." Now consider the flow of events concerning the Antichrist being referred to by one of his many names: the "vile person."

Daniel 11: Flow of Events

A king shall "fall," possibly by the sword. The leader that replaces him stays only a "few days" and is not removed in "anger or in battle." Then the "vile person"—the Antichrist — replaces him. This is the same flow of events we saw in the resolution of the riddles of Revelation 13 and 17, explaining "the beast that was, and is not, and yet is." But there is more.

From the Bottomless Pit

A detail given in Revelation 17 seems to explain why Daniel initially refers to the Antichrist as a king, and then his reference changes to the "vile person" when he comes back to life after suffering the "deadly wound." And this detail is as informative as it is disturbing.

> ⁸The beast that you saw was, and is not, and will ascend out of the bottomless pit <u>and go to perdition.</u>
> Revelation 17:8

Going back to Revelation 17 and the description of the Antichrist, we are told that what awakens within the body of the Antichrist after suffering the "deadly wound... will ascend out of the bottomless pit." It is not human. It comes from "out of the bottomless pit" and possesses him. This "bottomless pit" is the place God cast "the angels who sinned," delivering "them into chains of darkness, to be reserved for judgment," according to 2 Peter 2. But in Revelation 9, its prisoners are released back to the earth in a scene of smoke so great that "the sun and the air were darkened because of the smoke of the pit." More darkness added to the earth's darkest time.

A Decades-Old Kingdom

Knowing that the Antichrist is the sixth king in the succession of Beast Kingdom leaders tells us something very important. The Beast Kingdom exists in the Biblically indicated ruling structure for only a relatively short period before the Antichrist assumes the throne. Decades, not centuries. That is because there are only five kings before his rise. This is all-important. Although unquestionably powerful elements of it certainly must have existed for centuries outside its final biblical structure, we see from various Scriptures that the final Biblical ruling form of the Beast Kingdom is that of a "king" (single leader) along with ten sub-leaders (council) referred to by Isaiah as "princes," or leaders who ultimately become actual "kings" with a "kingdom." Now it gets interesting. Because this opens the door to roughly estimating how close the Antichrist is to assuming the throne.

To see why the Antichrist appears to now be present in the world, impacting world affairs in a very dark way, it is first necessary to gain a clear understanding of his abilities as noted in Scripture. Abilities that are steeped in deception and "dark sentences."

PART II

HOW WE KNOW THE
ANTICHRIST IS PRESENT

Chapter Six

A MAN OF DARK SENTENCES

When the Antichrist begins exerting influence over world affairs, it will be like none before him. Of Antichrist, Daniel 7:24 tells us that "His power shall be mighty, but not by his own power." He is supernaturally empowered by Satan, making him the most devious, deadly, and deceptive leader in world history. Essentially, his ideas come from the gurgling cauldron called hell. Perfected over centuries of dark agents studying mankind's weaknesses. Consider the following verses from the prophet Daniel that describe the result of satanic intervention on his behalf.

> 23 And in the latter time of their kingdom, when the transgressors are come to the full, a king of fierce countenance, and understanding dark sentences, shall stand up. 24 And his power shall be mighty, but not by his own power: and he shall destroy wonderfully, and shall prosper, and practise, and shall destroy the mighty and the holy people.

> 25 And through his policy also he shall cause craft to prosper in his hand; and he shall magnify himself in his heart, and by peace shall destroy many: he shall also stand up against the Prince of princes; but he shall be broken without hand. Daniel 8:23-25

Now let's go back to the original Hebrew to expand on these descriptions. In the first verse, he is described as "fierce." The adjective "az" is used to mean strong and mighty. But that word is combined with "countenance," which in the original Hebrew is the masculine noun "panim," meaning a person's face or presence. So whoever this person is, those in his presence have a sense they are dealing with a very strong person. A man who instills fear and respect just by looking at him.

Adding to that sense of awe is his ability to come up with plans that are a magnitude greater than others. This is conveyed when we are told he will understand "dark sentences." In the original Hebrew, that is conveyed by the feminine noun "hida." And this description of him is very significant relative to world events that began unfolding in the year 2020.

Strong's Concordance tells us that "hida" conveys amazing abilities that are beyond those of others. Those abilities include understanding difficult questions, riddles, and enigmatic questions. Concepts that perplex others are fully understood by him, enabling the Antichrist to use them to his advantage. This word also conveys his ability to understand dark and obscure utterances. This is a very significant power. Because in the art of witchcraft, words and dark artifacts have great meaning and power. Christians know that on a spiritual level, words can grant legal rights to demonic attacks. Understanding that the Antichrist is satanic to his core means that through his "understanding dark sentences," on an occult or witchcraft level, he is beyond even those most advanced in the dark arts. Knowing what words and demonically infested artifacts are most powerful in summoning the forces of hell.

At the end of the verse, after all these descriptions, we are told he "shall stand up." This means to firmly hold one's ground. The Hebrew verb "amad" here indicates "endure, take one's stand." In the next verse, we are told, "he shall destroy wonderfully." The verb "sahat" here indicates not only to destroy but to corrupt, ruin or decay." Indeed, this shows the effect he has on those around him. Essentially, men of decency bend to his wicked will. They are corrupted.

In line with that, in the final verse, we are told that "craft" will prosper. In the original Hebrew, this is the feminine noun "mirma," which indicates "deceit and treachery." He engages in great "deceit and treachery." This explains why "by peace he shall destroy many." And being the "bow" behind the arrows, he is able to bring peace without incurring blame for the wars, even though he is directly responsible. He deceives his victims. And if we remember our history, it was Adolf Hitler — an Antichrist prototype — who used the constant lure of peace to cause Britain and France to lower their guard while he grew in power. Allowing him the time he needed to become stronger militarily than they were.

In Daniel 7, we are perhaps given one of the methods he employs to deceive when we are told he has "a mouth speaking great things." All of this leads to the following result, according to Daniel: When the Antichrist rises to the throne of the Beast Kingdom, it will become "exceeding dreadful, whose teeth were of iron, and his nails of brass; which devoured, brake in pieces, and stamped the residue with his feet." So severely is he persecuting the saints that we are told, "I beheld, and the same horn made war with the saints, and prevailed against them." Many are martyred. 2 Thessalonians 2 tells us more about his supernatural power.

> [9]Even him, whose coming is after the working of Satan
> with all power and signs and lying wonders.

The power of the Antichrist comes directly from Satan. These "signs and lying wonders" are all part of the deception he will use to great advantage. The most significant one is given in Revelation 13. The same verse used to explain how he will be both the sixth and eighth kings. Just as the centerpiece of Christianity is the resurrection of Jesus Christ, the centerpiece of the Beast Kingdom will be the resurrection of the Antichrist.

> [3]And I saw one of his heads as it were wounded to death; and his deadly wound was healed: and all the world wondered after the beast.

> [4]And they worshipped the dragon which gave power unto the beast: and they worshipped the beast, saying, Who is like unto the beast? who is able to make war with him? Revelation 13:3-4

As mentioned previously, the "heads" in the verse are a succession of seven kings. We are being told one will suffer a "deadly wound" and come back to life. Such a resurrection from the dead (lying wonder) will empower him seductively over the minds of the lost. Also, the supernatural power of the Antichrist is augmented by that of a false religious leader. And their combined efforts will reap a harvest of souls on an unimaginable scale. Since a condemned generation looks for a sign, the Antichrist and his religious leader will supply many.

World Religious Leader

The Antichrist and the world religious leader are birds of a feather. According to Scripture, the religious leader also understands dark and obscure utterances. About his abilities, we are told in Revelation 13: "And he exerciseth all the power of the first beast before him, and causeth the earth and them which dwell therein to worship the first beast, whose deadly wound was healed."

Like the Antichrist, the world religious leader is also able to employ occult power. Incantations, words, and demonic objects of witchcraft empowered by Satan reach a level never before accomplished by a human. As such, the imprisoned world is treated to a supernatural show like never before. He does "great wonders, so that he maketh fire come down from heaven on the earth in the sight of men." He also advises the entire world to do something in honor of the Antichrist, who came back from the dead. And when the world does, it will be shocked by the result.

> ^{14}And deceiveth them that dwell on the earth by the means of those miracles which he had power to do in the sight of the beast; saying to them that dwell on the earth, that they should make an image to the beast, which had the wound by a sword, and did live.

> ^{15}And he had power to give life unto the image of the beast, that the image of the beast should both speak, and cause that as many as would not worship the image of the beast should be killed. Revelation 13:14-15

Conclusion

It will be a time of supernatural manifestations on earth like never before. And legions of the deceived will become willing workers for the Beast Kingdom, having been heavily indoctrinated in darkness at "universities." A "diverse" or "different" kind of kingdom led by the Antichrist, whom Scripture tells us will be "fierce," strong and mighty, and understand "dark sentences" (plans and schemes), problems that to others are riddles and enigmatic questions beyond their grasp. He will understand occult or witchcraft-type utterances that carry dark power. He will employ "craft," reaching a level of deceit and treachery beyond even that of the worst leaders in world history. Partly, this will be done by his having "a mouth speaking great things." Hitler, as the prototype Antichrist, possessed the same mesmerizing speaking abilities. And wherever his rule reaches (worldwide), there will be corruption, decay, and ruin. He will destroy on an unimaginable scale.

He will be joined by a world religious leader whose mission is to direct worship toward him. And as bad as the Antichrist is as he goes about killing people on a mass scale, the world religious leader will be focusing on their souls. Employing economic pressure to force them to take a mark on their bodies, signifying their acceptance of the Antichrist as a god. Those political activists today who work to cancel the livelihood of anyone opposing their dark anti-God agenda appear to be the first probes of the Beast Kingdom. Exploring how far it can push. They are those who will willingly serve the beast. Using strong economic pressure to force people to conform to their wicked will.

Because of his unmatched abilities to understand "craft" and "dark sentences," he will be able to develop and execute complicated plans. Plans that have an array of moving parts making them all fit together toward a multitude of dark goals. Historically unique plans such as the one that began unfolding in December 2019.

Chapter Seven

A BRILLIANT DARK PLAN: THE SIGN ANTICHRIST IS NOW ENGAGING THE WORLD

A s effective as the attacks on September 11th were in ushering in the age of surveillance within the United States and most of the West, it would be nothing compared to the unleashing of COVID-19 in December 2019 on the entire world. In a laboratory deep in China, more than a pandemic unfolded. But a multifaceted plan so brilliantly executed as to be astounding in its intricate detail and far-reaching impact. Indicating that someone possessing extraordinarily dark abilities and occult understandings has arrived on the world stage. A kind of calling card that the Antichrist is present in the New World Order. The Beast Kingdom.

Shredding the "Natural Origin" Theory

It was a virus produced in a lab, according to BioRxIv. An open-access preprint repository for the biological sciences who concluded that "it is highly likely that the SARS-CoV-2 virus that causes COVID-19 originated in a laboratory. The odds of a natural origin, according to the study, are placed at less than 1 in 100 million."[1] And the knowledge that it was manmade is all important. Had it been natural in origin, then claims that it was purposely released would be less credible. But knowing it was manmade opens the door wide to its release being done for a dark purpose. And from a very dark mind, understanding "dark sentences" and the art of "craft." Occult craft. Especially when its manmade origin is placed in context with the strange response to the virus from most Western nations. A response that cost untold hundreds of thousands of lives within nations most entangled within the New World Order's web of tentacles. Especially the United States. But that is only for starters.

A documentary on the COVID-19 pandemic called *Plandemic 2* is likely the most comprehensive set of informed accusations on the entire affair. It is a fact-rich presentation produced by Dr. David Martin. His impeccable credentials include being CEO of M-Cam Inc., an organization that advises over 160 nations on matters ranging from finance to trade to intangible assets. He was Chairman of Economic Innovation for the U.N. And his company has served as an advisor to numerous Central Banks, economic forums, and the World Bank. He has also worked with the U.S. Congress as well as the European Union. With these and many more credentials, he has been a frequent guest on shows such as CNBC and Bloomberg News. Until he began exposing the multitude of lies gathered around COVID-19.[2, 3]

With access to a mountain of facts collected over time through the course of his organization's business activities, Dr. Martin believes COVID-19 was and remains an act of biological warfare perpetrated on the human race.[4] Here is a brief sketch of a small part of the facts he presented to the European Union Parliament in 2023 on COVID-19.

The Corona virus was first identified in 1965 as an "infectious replaceable virus model." That wording means that it could be used to modify a series of human viral experiences. This also meant it showed the potential for use as a weapon. And this ability to be engineered and modified made it unique among viruses.[5] As a result of its malleable nature, Martin points to hundreds of published science studies between 1990 and 2018 whose consensus was that vaccines would not work on the Corona virus for the simple reason that it keeps changing over time.[6, 7] In addition to that staggering revelation, between those years there were other developments.

In 1990, Pfizer Pharmaceutical filed a patent for the spike protein.[8, 9] That would be the same "spike protein" the world was told was new in 2020. After studying the Corona virus between 1999 and 2002, a research facility at the University of North Carolina at Chapel Hill developed "an infectious replication defective clone of Corona virus." According to Martin, this labeling meant it could be modified as a weapon to target specific individual organs without collateral damage to other organs. And the one from the University was designed to target heart and lung tissue.[10, 11] This action of altering a virus to redirect it is called "gain of function." It is called that because it is being manipulated to have additional impacts or functions on the human body. In other words, gain of function represents very dark research.

In 2003, the United States Center for Disease Control (CDC) filed a patent for a specific SARS Corona virus isolated from humans. (Patent US7776521B1) The sequence was downloaded from China and filed in the United States. In 2005, this pathogen was labeled a bio-terrorism and bio-weapon platform technology.[12, 13] The initial sentences of the patent abstract read as follows:

> Disclosed herein is a newly isolated human coronavirus (SARS-CoV), the causative agent of severe acute respiratory syndrome (SARS). Also provided are the nucleic acid sequence of the SARS-CoV genome and the amino acid sequences of the SARS-CoV open reading frames...[14]

However, under U.S.C. S101: Subject of Eligibility: "A naturally occurring DNA segment is a product of nature and not patent eligible merely because it has been isolated." In other words, you can't patent elements of nature. And this makes sense. However, if the virus has been altered through "gain of function" research, then the altered version would no longer be considered naturally occurring, making it eligible for a patent. So as long as the virus was altered, then the CDC's patent is legal. However, if it were altered, then it would run into trouble elsewhere, becoming a violation of the production of biological weapons under international law. In light of these facts, not surprisingly, on May 14, 2007, the CDC filed a petition with the patent office under "Request for non-publication and certification under 35 U.S.C. S 122(b)(2)(b)(i) to keep the application private. For obvious reasons, the CDC did not want the implications of their patent to be discovered. At the same time, they also filed for a patent on its detection (PATENT US 7776521) as well as a kit to measure it.[15]

In 2012, Dr. Martin spoke before the European Union Parliament as an expert witness concerning biological patenting and if Europe should adopt a policy of allowing patents on biologically derived materials. Speaking forcefully against the weaponization of nature against humanity, he ended his talk with this grim warning: a bio-weapon release upon humanity was coming.[16] Later, in 2014, all "gain of function" research was terminated within the U.S. and transferred to Wuhan, China. In 2016, leading virologist Dr. Ralph Baric of the University of North Carolina stated in a presentation that the Wuhan Institute of Virology Virus I spike protein is poised for human emergence.[17] This would be the same Dr. Baric who, in 2005, gave a presentation titled: Biohacking a Corona Virus as an Enabling Technology for Bio-Warfare."[18]

In 2018, a new parlance entered the vernacular of the National Academy of Sciences when speaking on the subject of pandemics: That there would be an "accidental or intentional release of a respiratory pathogen."[19] Using that parlance, in April 2019, Moderna Pharmaceutical applied for four patents for an emergency use vaccine for the "accidental or intentional release of a respiratory pathogen." For a virus that was not yet in existence.[20]

In concluding his lengthy interview with the Internet information portal "Real London," Dr. Martin relayed a story related to his 2023 talk to the European Union Parliament. He said while in Brussels, he was approached by a man (unnamed) who handed him a "black envelope." Within it was a copy of a proposal from the US Department of Defense to identify contractors for the next pandemic.[21]

A Multitude of Dark Accomplishments

What COVID-19 darkly accomplished was to dramatically move world governments — especially the United States, which was likely the main target — much closer to totalitarian international control. It also created an environment to replace President Trump. A U.S. president who was antithetical to international control over the nation. Replacing him with a kind of vassal state leader taking orders from that "somewhere" President Wilson wrote about. It also laid the groundwork for the Great Reset. A financial move in line with the totalitarian financial control sought by the Beast Kingdom. It taught people to obey dictates relating to the outward display of something on their body to enter a store and engage in commerce. A clear forerunner to the mark of the Beast. It killed on a widespread scale. Something the Beast Kingdom seeks in its drive to reduce the world's population. A stated goal of those on the dark side of the political spectrum. And it manipulated billions of people across the globe to take a dangerous "vaccine" shot, allowing themselves to be injected with something new. Something that proved to be very dangerous to their health, while the major media acted in concert, withholding information on the effects of the shot. As well as withholding the consensus of science studies indicating a vaccine on a

Corona type virus was not even possible. It was as though a hidden hand guided the media into becoming accomplices to a great crime. It shut down churches across the nation. Establishing a government precedent of control over worship. All of these and more Beast Kingdom goals were accomplished.

There have been many dark minds over time who would have gladly enacted such a multipronged program. But they neither had the understanding nor the ability to do so. Such a level of understanding of "dark sentences" is reserved for the Antichrist. Whose power is not from himself but from Satan. And the ability to enact such a dark plan involves a multitude of helpers. As COVID-19 demonstrated, there are now legions in key positions nationally and internationally. Individuals indoctrinated in darkness from a multitude of universities. Further indicating the time for the Antichrist has arrived. All of which resulted in a series of responses to COVID-19 that not only cost more lives, but were methodical and coordinated in closing down public life and the economic structures of entire nations. Resulting in spiraling suicide rates as well as other physical and psychological damage.

The Dark Response

The COVID-19 response was the most manipulative one in the history of infectious diseases. Characterized by an unending series of coordinated lies from governments, medical associations, the media, and international agencies.[22] A clear indication of the widespread nature of the Beast Kingdom's reach across the globe. There were many "firsts" when it came to the COVID-19 pandemic. It was a first for medical protocols not to be based on successful treatments used by front-line physicians. It was a first for bureaucracies to take the lead instead of seasoned medical personnel.[23]

It was also a first for the major media to appoint themselves as the sole source of truthful information on a pandemic. All dedicated to a single-minded narrative that, if crossed, resulted in consequences for the violator. Websites releasing information on effective treatments being used by highly credentialed and experienced clinical doctors were taken down. It was also a first for experts in the field of infectious diseases to be demonized for not conforming to an official narrative. A narrative that had more in common with political science than medical science. A first for destroying the careers of top experts in the fields of virology, infectious diseases, pulmonary critical care, and epidemiology who dared to practice the time-tested scientific method of critical analysis. In other words, employing their medical observations to disagree with the official narrative. It was a first for demonizing a top whistleblower from a pharmaceutical company for blowing the whistle on a dangerous vaccine. That would be an ex-chief scientist and vice president for the science division of Pfizer Pharmaceutical.[24]

Precedents for dealing with pandemics were completely ignored. From public health responses to American legal tradition and medical knowledge relating to respiratory viruses, all were ignored in favor of never-before-tried draconian decrees. As though the real goal was to teach the people of the world extreme obedience. A Beast Kingdom favorite. And the sudden appearance of the pandemic in December 2019 was no excuse for such responses. Every pandemic in history has been a surprise. That is their nature. And the one that began appearing in December 2019 was no different. However, it seems that not everyone was surprised by its appearance. Coincidentally, between January and August 2019, elements in the U.S. government ran a pandemic response exercise called "Crimson Contagion."

Crimson Contagion was a government exercise that involved a large number of public-sector agencies and private-sector associations, plus participation from all fifty states. The head of the operation was Robert Kadlec. As the Assistant Secretary of Health and Human Resources under the Trump Administration, he is also thought to be a CIA agent.[25] The exercise postulated the following disease scenario: A respiratory virus begins in China and spreads around the world through air travelers. Then, 47 days later, the World Health Organization declares a pandemic. If this sounds familiar, it should. It is essentially what began unfolding only four months later.[26] What a coincidence!

A Beastly Response

The official response to the virus started with a lie. The government and media (one and the same) promoted the narrative that the virus mutated into existence in the dark recesses of a dirty food market in Wuhan, China. Adding the detail that the dirty market was selling bats for consumption.[27] A perfect storyline for Western consumption. Creating a level of disgust that would explain everything. People eating dirty bats caused the virus to develop! After that narrative was spread, the united media's second narrative began almost immediately. One designed to generate unbridled fear across the nation.

True to form, major media outlets — which lost their independence decades earlier to that unseen force — were used to generate a drumbeat of fear. Some major media outlets even kept a death count on their screens just in case a person watching happened upon a moment of peace. Once fear was deeply ingrained, the demands started. The first was that a mask had to be worn. This mask, the worried masses were told, was for everyone's protection. However, early on, it was indicated by the Center for Disease Control (CDC) that masks were not useful. But that little tidbit was quickly forgotten. And anyone could see why masks did not work. Air passed easily in and out around the sides, providing no protection. But the false narrative became a form of holy gospel that no one dared challenge for fear of being excommunicated for the sin of not caring. Not coincidentally, the forced wearing of masks to enter stores for commerce was eerily in line with something the future holds, according to Revelation 13. The requirement of wearing something associated with the Antichrist to buy or sell. The whole mask affair was a brilliant dry run.

But the mask was only for those venturing out from the relative safety of their homes. That is because entire populations of nations were placed in "lockdown." A term typically used for prison revolts and not free people. Another dry run. The lockdowns took away basic human freedom as well as dignity. Creating a new sense of government dependency even within the most independent souls. Losing the right to work, shop, and play. In other words, losing the right to simply live life. Obedience was the essential ingredient demanded by their new masters. And the whole affair was directly in conflict with the concept of developing natural immunity. An approach that had worked well for societies ever since men lived in caves.

And like the mask narrative, major media, in unison, added lockdowns to their gospel. Taking on the façade of a holy crusade dedicated to protecting people. When, in reality, it robbed the nation of its natural immunity while destroying the economy and the personal freedom and finances of tens of millions. Not to mention causing serious mental health issues. Yet none of the major media outlets questioned the absurd dictates. Like mindless zombies, they simply followed the narrative. A strange single-mindedness that Revelation 17 tells us the ten kings/princes will share in support of the Beast and his kingdom.

Another false narrative promoted by these ministries of truth — working so closely with the government that no light between them could be seen — was that there was no medical treatment for COVID-19. None. The public was on their own if they contracted it. And with constant fear-mongering, many thought they would quickly be pushing up roses should they contract the virus. However, that lie was a deadly one. As the virus progressed, front-line clinics reported on an assortment of drug treatments that were lowering the death toll. One such treatment was the powerful antibiotic Z-PAC, which appeared to kill the infection associated with COVID-19. Allowing the body to deal more effectively with the virus. This author received a Z-PAC for both COVID-19 and the Omecron variants. In both cases, recovery began only hours later.

Other drugs, such as hydroxylchloroquine, were also helping patients. Doctors on the front lines were reporting favorable results.[28] Certainly better than doing nothing. Then a study was done giving COVID-19 patients the drug. According to a doctor friend of mine, all the patients given the drug were already on the brink of death when it was administered. He was insinuating that the study was rigged. Then, after all the patients in the study died, the drug was branded dangerous. Despite front-line clinics reporting good results as long as it was administered immediately! With the negative results of the "study," doctors were then banned from administering it to their patients. And the ministries of truth then kicked in again. Almost gleefully spreading the news that those given the drug had all died. Never mentioning the fact that they were already on the brink of death when it was given! This sustained their narrative of hopelessness. A narrative that appeared to be one dictated to them from that "something" located "somewhere." Then, when yet another drug was showing promising results, they kicked into gear again. But this time taking a slightly different approach.

It was reported that a deworming drug called Ivermectin was having a positive impact on the virus.[29] In this case, the approach was to point out that the drug was also used on animals. The propaganda line went something like this: "Don't take a drug that's meant for animals!" Being dedicated to hopelessness, they never mentioned that the drug had been safely used by humans for decades! Also left out was the detail that dozens of drugs are used both by humans and animals to treat illness. But such a context would not have been in line with their narrative of fear and hopelessness. However, the orchestration of hopeless circumstances should not have been a surprise. It was exactly what was predicted years earlier by Henry Kissinger. A major New World Order proponent who indicated such a method could be used for gaining control over whole populations. A necessary requirement to advance the goal of a one-world government. According to Kissinger, if the American people were...

> "...told that there were an outside threat from beyond, whether real or promulgated, that threatened our very existence. It is then that all peoples of the world will plead to deliver them from this evil. The one thing every man fears is the unknown. When presented with this scenario, individual rights will be willingly relinquished for the guarantee of their well-being granted to them by the World Government... a New World Order."[30]

The threat Kissinger foretold was found in COVID-19. A threat that had to be ginned up to accomplish a dark agenda. And one of the leading actors behind it all was the World Health Organization (WHO). An international one-world government organization, whose first Director General, Mr. Brock Chisholm, had the following to say concerning the organization's goals:

> "To achieve world government, it is necessary to remove from the minds of men, their individualism, loyalty to family traditions, national patriotism and religious dogmas."[31]

How ending "individualism, loyalty to family traditions, national patriotism and religious dogmas" promotes the health and well-being of people across the globe is anyone's guess. But it does indicate the type of people being placed over the health of countless people in the world. Individuals appearing more interested in the advancement of dark political goals than health and well-being. Perfectly in line with the overall COVID-19 national and international government responses. And Chisholm would not be the only strange character placed in that position. Billionaire Bill Gates, whose influence over WHO directors is great due to the massive funding he provides, succeeded in placing another winner in that key position as director just before COVID-19 was released. That would be Ethiopian Marxist revolutionary Tedros Adhanom Ghebreyesus.[32]

Behind all of the fear-mongering, mask-wearing, lockdowns, and medicines being withheld was something much bigger than even the pandemic. And possibly one of the main reasons the virus was released. The establishment of a rationale for getting something injected into the bodies of billions of people across the world at the same time. A brilliantly dark plan!

Why the World Was Attacked

According to federal law, vaccines cannot be rushed unless certain conditions are met. The first is that there is a pandemic on the loose, endangering the American people. With the unleashing of COVID-19, that requirement was fulfilled. But the second requirement is trickier. There must not be any medicines available to combat the virus. If it is reported that a drug or drugs (which was the case with COVID-19) were actually helping address a pandemic, then no emergency order can be granted. And then no rushed "vaccine" will be allowed.[33] That seems to explain why major media outlets were instructed to promote the narrative of hopelessness and attack drugs that were saving lives. All demonstrating the behavior of a Beast Kingdom tentacle. Transformed from a free press into a guild of dark messengers willing to withhold information at the expense of countless lives.

There appear to have been several reasons why the COVID-19 virus was unleashed on the world. Because behind every dark plan, there is a purpose. The first appears to be to establish a rationale to justify injecting billions of people across the globe with a substance. World population reduction would be another goal. A goal indicated by various powerful individuals. And indicated by a dark message delivered decades ago, covered in the chapter titled "Thelemic Occult Magick." Another purpose appears to be directly related to the 2020 U.S. presidential election. The goal of defeating President Trump in his bid for re-election. And then there is the Great Reset. The goal of taking control over the financial lives of people to a degree only dreamed of by dictators. Also, the release of COVID-19 taught the public to place something on their bodies to engage in commerce. All of which is a forerunner of Revelation 13. It set the precedent of shutting down churches as well as locking down entire populations. For their good, of course. The release of COVID-19 accomplished a multitude of dark plans. Brilliant from a demonic perspective. Indicating it was the brainchild of someone profoundly knowledgeable in the dark arts.

The Vaccine: Obedience to Death

The development of a vaccine is a long, complex process, often lasting 10–15 years. And for good reason. They can prove dangerous if not vetted properly. Regulation of vaccine production began in 1902, when Congress passed the Biologics Control Act. Written to "regulate the sale of viruses, serums, toxins, and analogous products."[34] However, when it came to the COVID-19 "vaccine," the process was shortened to 12 months. Essentially, developing a "vaccine" in a hurry for a virus that a multitude of science studies indicated was not possible. Apparently, "following the science" is a selective process. One of the results was the creation of a whole new acronym, SADS. Sudden Adult Death Syndrome. Whose correlation to the vaccine rollout is as undeniable as it is sad.[35] Perfectly healthy adults suddenly dropped dead. But that was only for starters.

Frankenstein's Lab

In a room set aside for prepping the deceased for viewing, an embalmer makes a startling discovery. After attempting numerous times to inject embalming fluid into the artery system of the subject, she discovers that something appears to be blocking it from flowing through. Opening up some of the main arteries in the body, she makes a gruesome discovery. From within the subject's body, she removes a three-foot-long rubbery strand. Shocked by what she finds, she begins exploring further. Soon she discovers that the subject's whole artery system is filled with these strands. And they are not blood clots. But some Frankenstein-like rubbery substances that have no business being in a human body. However, it will not be a one-time experience. But the beginning of a horrifying new norm. And not just for her.[36]

At the 2022 convention for embalmers, the subject of long rubbery strands suddenly being found in cadavers would come up. In a room of over one hundred embalmers from across the United States, almost all agreed on seeing these strange fibers coming out of people. And all also agree that it is something they have never before seen. Dramatically changing the industry from one of routine work days to one filled with horrifying discoveries. They agree that these strange rubbery strands started appearing sometime in mid-2021.[37] Coincidentally, after the "vaccines" started mass distribution. One funeral director estimated that these mystery clots have suddenly started appearing in 50–70 percent of the cadavers being serviced at his facility.[38] But embalmers are not the only industry experiencing something new.

Miscarriages & Stillbirths

At a hospital in Fresno, California, a nurse observes something strange. Whereas before the year 2021, the average number of stillbirths at the hospital numbered about 2-3 over two months. After the vaccine's distribution, the number suddenly exploded to an average of 22 per month. A massive increase! Duty-bound, she brings this dramatic spike data to her supervisor. He shows no interest. Instead, the hospital sought to hide the terrifying information. As such, the nurse leaks a memo circulating in the hospital concerning the spike in stillbirths to the media.[39] Mainstream media obediently ignores it. But she's not the only one seeing the impact on mothers and their babies.

Dr. James Thorp, a board-certified OBGYN who sees thousands of patients a year, also saw a massive spike in his patients experiencing miscarriages and stillbirths. A new reality since the mass COVID-19 vaccines were issued. Disturbed by what he was seeing, he obtained vaccine manufacturer Pfizer's data from the limited testing of their shot. In those pages, he discovers why his practice has had a spike in deadly outcomes for his patients.[40]

Pfizer's test data revealed that a staggering 80% of pregnant women given the vaccine experienced miscarriages. Shocked by the data, the doctor was quoted as saying: "The federal government, the CDC, and the FDA—they're corrupt. They sat on that data."[41] More agencies that embrace the morals of the unseen kingdom. As multiple sources of anecdotal information sketch an increasingly gruesome picture, confirmation of the resulting death toll comes from the Society of Actuaries.

In the year 2022, the Society of Actuaries Research Institute released its 2021 report on deaths in the United States. In Table 4 on page 6 of their report, one of the most staggering pieces of data on mortality numbers ever is found. For the year 2021 — the first year the vaccines were widely distributed — the mortality rate "excluding COVID-19" compared to expected deaths was calculated at 209%![42] More than a doubling of the death rate. The statistic reflects combined age groups and both sexes. But perhaps none of this should be a surprise.

Bill Gates, whose influence relative to vaccines appears out of place to his computer software background, has not only bought great influence over the direction of the World Health Organization, but also let slip during a 2020 Ted Talk one of the reasons he is so interested in the World Health Organization. Asserting that:

> "If we do a really great job on new vaccines, health care, and reproductive health services, we could lower [the world population] by ten or fifteen percent."[43]

But this is strange. Because if the improvement of "new vaccines, health care, and reproductive services" was to be beneficial to the world's population, then there should be an actual increase in healthy births. Not a decline. Unless the real goal is population reduction. But the powerful billionaire's influence had another impact. Along with John Hopkins University and the World Economic Forum, the Bill and Melinda Gates Foundation cosponsored the Event 201 Exercise. A simulation dry run of "a series of dramatic, scenario-based facilitated discussions, confronting difficult, true-to-life dilemmas associated with response to... a pandemic."[44] In other words, another pandemic dry run only months before COVID-19 was released.

With the beneficial nature of "new vaccines, health care, and re-productive services" being defined as having the potential to reduce the world population by "ten to fifteen percent," the World Health Organization is seeking extraordinary emergency powers over the affairs of nations. In line with these new powers, it is also changing its prime directive away from being implemented "with full respect for the dignity, human rights, and fundamental freedoms of persons." A noble ideal. To be replaced with "principles of equity, inclusivity, and coherence." Indicating they can force their version of fairness on individuals as they deem necessary.[45] And if all of this doesn't yet appear to have come out of a Frankenstein-type laboratory, then perhaps the next item will.

The Department of Homeland Security, always looking for a way to track the American people, filed a patent request for a product using a bioluminescent material. A material used to internally mark people who take the next vaccine for the next pandemic. Appropriately named the "Luciferase Mark," it will use "bioluminescent quantum dots" to track people's medical data.[46] Perhaps an indication that another virus is coming. And indicating that those unwilling to allow a substance to be injected into their bodies will face a form of segregation within society. Approved humans can be identified by an internal marker. Another forerunner to the coming requirement of having a mark on the right hand or forehead to buy or sell.

The unleashing of COVID-19 set a precedent for extreme control over people. And whoever was behind it had as much concern for human life as Scripture tells us the Antichrist will. Exactly what devious substance, if any, was included in some vaccines is unknown. But two things are known: First, the push to get an emergency order to produce the vaccines involved the withholding of medicines that frontline clinics reported were helping to reduce the death rate. That action in itself represents genocide. Indicating not only that moral degenerates were behind it but also fully revealing the corrupt nature of major media in the U.S. and Western Europe. Willing accomplices to one of the crimes of the century. All of which appears to be in line with reducing the world's population. But it also shows something else.

The release of COVID-19 was so effective in manipulating the people of the world, especially in the West, removing their freedom and forcing them to outwardly display something (mask) which acted as a sign allowing commerce, that it was a dark masterpiece beyond anything found in the history books. An effort that included suppressing medicine and information at the cost of countless lives in the U.S. alone. Demonstrating a level of power never before seen on a worldwide level. Also, demonstrating Beast Kingdom-type morals and ethics. And that is a game changer, indicating someone of extraordinary dark understanding is now on the scene. But all of this was only for starters. There appear to have been other goals accomplished by its release.

The 2020 Presidential Election

The administration of President Trump was to the Beast Kingdom what Kryptonite is to Superman. The President of the United States is the most powerful leader on earth. And Trump's America First policy was a complete reversal of the internationalism driving U.S. policy since the days of Woodrow Wilson. It was completely in contradiction with the goals of the many international organizations set up to encourage and support a borderless world. As well as pushing internationalism in place of patriotism. There, too, his policies were anathema.

By aggressively addressing the invasion at the southern border, he was not only reversing a major policy goal of the Beast Kingdom for the United States, but also setting an example for a host of other leaders to follow. Effectively, unraveling years of efforts by the Beast Kingdom to wreak havoc and weaken the Western nations. Through chaos and havoc, more control can be obtained.

The southern border has been a magnet for criminals to enter the United States to conduct profitable business within its wealthy borders. While in the meantime accomplishing the Beast Kingdom's goal of death and chaos caused by high crime. It also provides a portal of entry for massive amounts of drugs to come in, bringing about more chaos, countless deaths, and destroying families. In just a single year, 100 suspects on the FBI terror watch list were caught attempting to cross the border.[47] And only a small percentage of illegal border crossings are detained. Indicating that a large number of foreign fighters have been coming into the U.S. for years. But there appears to be another reason for the Beast Kingdom wanting open borders for the Western nations.

In the chapter titled "Trojan Horses," the case is made as to how the Antichrist completes the process of taking down the most powerful nations on earth, including the United States. A scenario that is laid out by considering the words of the prophets Isaiah, Joel, Zephaniah, and John in Revelation. The conclusion in that chapter represents staggering consequences for the West. And open borders are essential for this event to unfold as foretold by those prophets.

Opposing Moloch

One of the most significant actions that a U.S. president can engage in is the selection of Supreme Court justices. Their impact on human life and freedom often exceeds that of both Congress and the President. It would be there that Trump would receive three slots to fill during his first term, creating a majority of justices who eventually overturned Roe v. Wade. The Supreme Court's horrific ruling on abortion that resulted in the deaths of millions of babies. Death of the most innocent, pleasing the wicked god Moloch and those running the Beast Kingdom.

Part of the reason the Beast Kingdom seeks to sew chaos and death within the United States is to weaken it. A weakened country is easier to control. But Trump's approach to the U.S. economy began reversing years of policies that stifled economic growth and opportunity. And with the economy roaring going into the 2020 election year, it was clear that the odds of defeating him through free and fair elections were slim. Yet Trump represented an enemy of the Beast Kingdom that had to be destroyed. It is here, too, that the release of COVID-19 fulfilled another major goal of the Beast Kingdom.

Destroy Trump!

Immediately after the shocking election victory of Donald Trump to the presidency in 2016, it appears the New World Order/Beast Kingdom gave the order for him to either be killed or his presidency destroyed. Having seen the results of John F. Kennedy challenging the powers that be, Trump took a different approach to his safety during his presidency. Hiring his own security detail and paying them large amounts of money to protect him. Something no previous president thought was necessary for their personal safety.[48] True to form, this incredible fact would be withheld from the American people by the corrupted mainstream media. Obviously, Trump knew something about the forces arrayed against him. Forces so dark and powerful that even a U.S. president was not safe. The same hidden power that, over a hundred years earlier, another president described in dire terms. The same less organized entity that probably was behind the assassination attempt against President Andrew Jackson.

By the time Trump was elected, it had become clear that the powerful kingdom Wilson wrote about in 1913 had evolved into a worldwide kingdom, with its dark tentacles extending into the power centers of nations across the world. Especially within the Western nations, whose powerful media corporations — filled with individuals indoctrinated to oppose Scripture — were used as ministries spreading darkness not only within the United States and the West but across the entire globe, directly confronting scriptural values wherever they could be found. These efforts against Trump by the New World Order — the Beast Kingdom — were the first sign that Trump was not a part of it. The next sign would come quickly.

A natural question arises from the fact that Trump hired his own security force at the outset of his administration. Why didn't he simply task the FBI with tracking down any organized threats against him? Along with the Secret Service, that is part of their job description. As his presidency unfolded, the answer to that question would become obvious. The FBI was compromised. As the Trump presidency unfolded, one revelation after another would come out that the FBI was engaged in a conspiracy to undermine his presidency.[49, 50] And by the end of his four years in office, their reputation would be left in tatters with that segment of America that receives real information.

Detailing all of the attacks against the Trump presidency is beyond the scope of this chapter. But the point needs to be made that his presidency experienced a level of attack never before seen against an American president. Even Richard Nixon never experienced the degree of organized action against him from within his own government. And the answer to why this happened is two-fold. First, he sought to reverse the drive toward a one-world government that had been the mainstay of U.S. policy for decades and the thrust of the Beast Kingdom's drive for control over a nation. And, secondly, because the New World Order — the Beast Kingdom — had grown in power within the United States, controlling a major political party —the Democratic Party — and being able to direct it to do its bidding. But its dark tentacles were not limited there. In the end, all of the efforts against his presidency would fail. Meaning something dramatic had to be done to stop him from winning a second term. And the unleashing of COVID-19 would provide the cover.

The 2020 Presidential Election

The 2020 presidential election in the United States was the first where mail-in voting played a major role. After the election was over, notable election observers pointed out a multitude of voting irregularities, including mass stuffing of ballot boxes, votes suddenly reversing from Trump to Biden on TV as people watched, and blackouts on vote counting with Trump leading in all swing states by massive margins, only to have those leads suddenly disappear upon reopening counting. Security footage showing shady activity taking place after Trump poll watchers were told to leave. Extended recounts, the unceremonious dismissal of legal challenges, and a host of other activities and irregularities. After the election was over, it was discovered that a powerful group, including the media, billionaires, NGOs, and even government officials, colluded to "fortify" the election. In other words, interfere with it. A study done by conservative documentary producer Dinesh D'Souza using cell phone tracking data ended with the conclusion that the volume of votes likely stolen on behalf of Biden in key states, limited only to using the mail-in ballot boxes, was enough to swing the election in each of those states and the presidency.

Considering the extent to which agencies such as the FBI went to undermine the Trump presidency, it is not difficult to believe there was an organized effort to steal votes on behalf of Biden in the 2020 election. With what may have been a tacit understanding that the FBI would look away. We may never know what is true and what is not true concerning allegations of vote rigging, FBI collusion, and vote theft. But one thing is certain. With the widespread use of mail-in voting, the 2020 election was fraught with issues. And COVID-19 was used as an excuse to implement that new system. Another brilliant facet of a dark plan!

Then, after "winning" the presidency, President Biden used his Department of "Justice" to indict former President Trump. His main political opponent. An action common in banana republics. With such brazen corruption of law enforcement agencies for all to see, on behalf of a president who appears to be nothing more than a puppet, it is becoming apparent that a very dark force has taken over the most important institutions in America. And such corruption is the natural byproduct of wherever the tentacles of the Beast Kingdom touch.

The Great Reset

There has been increasing talk within informed circles of a coming Great Reset. An all-encompassing term used to describe a complete makeover of the world into a godless totalitarian kingdom. Stripping populations of basic human rights in an effort to bind them under a heavy new authority. An authority that seeks to impose a form of modern slavery on a truncated population. Removing financial freedom as well as freedom of speech and assembly. A system of godless indoctrination in place of education. A process already far along on the road to paganism. All good descriptions and goals of the Beast Kingdom. A hidden kingdom whose unrelenting tentacles enter and undermine the moral and ethical integrity of a multitude of major institutions. An entity whose goals not only include totalitarian control over every aspect of individual life but intimately intertwine it with an anti-God agenda. Or, put another way, an anti-Christ agenda. A sure sign of its dark spiritual roots.

COVID-19 was also a tool used to advance the Great Reset. A move to achieve total control over the individual by mandating lockdowns and the wearing of a worthless mask in order to engage in commerce. Policies that inevitably produced broken supply chains, causing shortages and high costs. Combined with flooding the financial system with literally trillions of U.S. dollars given away en masse. Resulting in the highest inflation in decades and the destruction of the work ethic for millions. All dramatically undermining the financial condition of the average citizen.

The Great Reset could not move forward without the removal of a real American president. One not controlled by the New World Order/ Beast Kingdom. COVID-19 was successfully used to remove that president. Replacing him in the White House with a man following orders. Orders that entail actions that undermine the sovereignty of the United States. Directing the southern border to be left wide open for a mass invasion. Allowing deadly drugs and terrorist cells to enter the nation. Demonstrating presidential loyalty placed "somewhere" to "something" outside America. A vassal state president directing the U.S. military according to the dictates of the unseen kingdom. Engaging the United States in wars that in no way protect America or advance the cause of peace and freedom.

The Great Reset involves "climate change" policies driven by the same fear tactics employed during COVID-19. Suppressing notable scientific critics in the same way scientists critical of the vaccine were suppressed or had their reputations damaged. A climate "threat" used to seek a tax on carbon and bans on fertilizers producing food shortages. The driving force behind shuttering energy production.

The Great Reset also includes the drive to replace the freedom derived from a paper dollar with a digital one. Allowing the U.S. government to track and even control individual spending habits. As well as the ability to create more dollars by simply adding a zero. The new Central Bank Digital Currency (CBDC) may explain why the U.S. government allowed Bitcoin to go as far as it has. A true case study before the introduction of CBDC.

But for CBDC to be implemented, there are some obstacles standing in the way. The New World Order/Beast Kingdom would like only a few megabanks for easier control. A consolidation of a major industry just as has been done in the major media industry. But although a small number of monolithic banks account for the vast majority of transactions, there are still a large number of regional and local banks that afford people a choice. And such a choice reduces the ability for total control. In testimony before Congress, the Treasury Secretary telegraphed the approach to be taken in dealing with this problem. Making it clear that the government would only guarantee all deposits exceeding the $250,000 guarantee amount at the megabanks. Drawing a sharp rebuke from the Independent Community Bankers of America for effectively undermining regional banks by causing large depositors to leave for the mega banks.[51]

The Great Reset includes a proxy war in Ukraine. A strange war if there ever was one that actually started back in January 2014. When the U.S. government, under Barack Obama, overthrew the democratically elected government of Ukraine in what was called a "color revolution." The U.S. media — a tentacle of the Beast Kingdom — obediently obfuscated the fact that a C.I.A. coup took place in Ukraine, destabilizing the region. Immediately after the coup, a C.I.A. puppet regime was put in place. And with Nobel Peace Prize winner Barack Obama's approval, it began training anti-Russian militias in Ukraine along its border with

Russia. One such group, the Neo-Nazi Azov Battalion, gained a reputation for attacking Russian-speaking villages inside Ukraine. Where innocent people were killed for the crime of being Russian.[52] Something the German Nazis would have understood. With such antagonisms, it is difficult to believe the Obama regime did not know its actions would eventually lead to a war between Russia and Ukraine. But why would they seek to start a new war? Part of the answer may be related to the Great Reset.

Such a war, wherein Russia invades Ukraine to prevent them from joining NATO, has certainly been war-gamed. Clearly, such gaming included the imposition of severe sanctions against Russian commodities and the confiscation of their wealth as punishment. With Russia possessing more natural resources than any other nation on earth, such sanctions would be certain to bring financial distress to many quarters, furthering the Great Reset. But there is probably another reason for antagonizing Russia. That is to undermine Russian President Putin because he is apparently not a part of the New World Order/Beast Kingdom. This conclusion is based on his anti-gay, anti-lesbian, and anti-transgender laws and the traditional marriage position of his government. And we can be certain that no Beast Kingdom puppet or ally would dare support Biblical marriage.

COVID-19: A Very Dark Sentence

As a forerunner of the Antichrist, Adolf Hitler brought death and destruction to the European continent. And as Panzer divisions were rolling across the plains of Europe, deep in the Far East, Hideki Tojo, the warlord of Japan, went about doing the same. But as bad as their actions were, the release of COVID-19 was an attack against the entire world in a single blow. One perfectly placed strategic blow. Especially against the Western nations. Never before has there been anything like it unleashed with such precision to achieve a multitude of sinister goals. And forces aligned with the New World Order/Beast Kingdom took full advantage of it. A brilliant conquering without the use of a military army. Instead, an army of internationalists, the media, the government, major medical institutions, and a host of other assets were used to bring the world to its knees. But such an incredibly successful dark plan starts in the mind of a single man. And in this case, a man of such dark understandings as to be unique. Able to juggle multiple parts of the same plan with perfection. Bringing about a new level of control and bringing the Great Reset vastly closer to completion.

As much as the multifaceted planned release of COVID-19 indicates an individual of "dark sentences" has appeared on the world stage, there is another reason to believe the Antichrist is at or near the Beast Kingdom throne. And that has to do with estimating the age of the Beast Kingdom by estimating when it reached its final Biblical ruling form. This is not to say elements of it were not around long before that seminal moment. As a hidden kingdom, such an estimation can only be that — an estimate. But there are reasons to believe that what had previously been a confederacy of dark individuals, aligned for a multitude of motives, finally assumed it's Biblically indicated ruling structure sometime around the year 1900. Which, if true, makes it likely that the sixth king is very close to his throne.

Chapter Eight

THE EARLY 1900S: WHEN THE BEAST KINGDOM REACHED ITS BIBLICAL FORM?

ithin the ranks of any military force, an act of insubordination is considered a very serious offense. So much so that it can end the career of a soldier. The reason why is clear. Such an act undermines the chain of command. And this can lead to disaster on the battlefield. Therefore, the command authority of senior officers is sacrosanct. To win battles, power must be focused. And to focus power, a single person must be in charge. A person that everyone else is required to obey. A good example is the D-Day invasion of Nazi Europe in 1944.[1]

It was granted to General Eisenhower to be the Supreme Commander of Operation Overlord. The Allied invasion of Nazi Europe. Even though it was a massively large enterprise involving multiple nations and countless generals. Because more than one leader results in conflicting orders that diffuse or even negate the power of an organization. And that can bring disaster. This is also true for the projection of political power.

For a group of powerful people to succeed in taking over the most significant element of a nation's economy — assuming such great power as to be able to move the economy and stock market of a nation — their efforts must be highly focused. And that means there must be someone clearly at the top directing all resources available toward a single-minded objective. Someone who has the final word. A person who can settle differences in strategy and execution. A leader. A king.

Typically such leaders have a powerful group under them. In the case of Eisenhower, he had an array of generals from the various branches of the American, Canadian, and British militaries. Their roles were to offer advice, and they were influential. But once the order was given, they fell in line and executed it even if they had a different idea of what should be done. Such a structure is common within any group that successfully exerts power and influence. And the New World Order/Beast Kingdom should be no different. According to Scripture, it essentially has the same type of ruling structure.

The scriptural case was presented in the chapter titled "The Sixth King" that the Beast Kingdom has a succession of "kings." Leaders who almost certainly will have the final word since they are referred to in Scripture as "kings." But we also saw in the chapter titled "The Ten Kings" that there are sub-leaders or a council below these "kings." A group of ten powerful leaders referred to in Isaiah 10 by the Antichrist as his "princes." These ten have significant power within the Beast Kingdom. But there is only one king. And although Scripture tells us the ten chose the beast kings. Once chosen, all others would then be obligated to obey him. This is the essence of focused power. And an absolute necessity if the Beast Kingdom was to score any great achievements.

Orderly Ruling Structure

Since the Beast Kingdom has a succession of kings and a powerful group of ten sub-leaders — possibly a council of some kind before having literal kingdoms to rule — we can see that this is its Biblical ruling structure. This is not to say disorganized elements of it did not exist before it formed into its biblically indicated ruling structure. Undoubtedly, those elements did exist, likely for a long time. But to take a stab at when the beast kingdom finally evolved into its Biblical ruling structure with kings ruling it is very significant. Because the Antichrist will be its sixth king. So to pin down a general time frame, we are looking for when it accomplished a major objective that had previously eluded it. Indicating a newly acquired ability to focus power, which typically indicates better leadership. To do this, we must go back to the early 1800s and the efforts made by powerful forces to control the United States currency, banking system, economy, and stock market. Essentially, control America!

Central Banks

Privately owned central banks provide the greatest economic power and leverage over a nation. They control the money supply like a dam controls the flow of water. When the money supply contracts so too will economic activity and the stock market. Open it wide, and the flow of money brings greater economic activity, pushing up the stock market and eventually inflation. It is the ultimate economic control lever over a nation. Capable of bringing great wealth to those in control. That the New World Order/Beast Kingdom would strive to possess such power goes without saying. The most powerful banker in world history summed up that power long ago.

> "Give me control over a nation's currency, and I care not who makes its laws. Mayer Amschel Rothschild (1743–1812)"[2]

The Rothschild family of bankers is known in history for literally controlling nations through their banking empire. So there is little doubt that ultimately the family of the world's first bankers would be intensely interested in extending its reach into the central banks of nations through their surrogates. They certainly had the money to make a serious effort. And as powerful as the Rothschild banking empire was before central banks. Imagine how supercharged that power became afterward. The year Mayer Rothschild gave that quote was 1790. The next year, the First Bank of the United States was established.

Andrew Jackson's Bank Battle

The history of a central bank in the United States starts in 1791, when George Washington and Alexander Hamilton created a central depository for federal funds directly controlled by the U.S. government. However, to get it through Congress, it was necessary to limit its charter to 20 years. In 1811, when the bank's charter came to an end, it was not extended. The reason it was not extended was that there was too much political opposition in the U.S. And it is clear that the forces wanting to maintain it were not organized enough to get the extension. But the battle over a central bank was just beginning in America. Five years later, in 1816, banking forces would once again muster the political support necessary to create another central bank. This one was called the Second Bank of the United States. But those involved in establishing it did not see a coming event that would be a major stumbling block. The election of General Andrew Jackson to the presidency.[3]

As a common man's president, Jackson was hated by the elites of the nation. By no measure was he a Rothschild president. And he appeared to instinctively understand that a central bank was primarily helpful to the powerful and not the common man. Using the common man's money to build personal wealth and then leaving the little guy holding the bag when things go wrong. If that sounds familiar, it should. It is what has been happening in the United States and many other countries around the world for some time now. The 2008 banking bailout of the rich and powerful is a prime example.

Even before the Second Bank of the United States' charter was set to expire, Jackson began taking steps to effectively kill it. Immediately after his inauguration, he started an investigation into the practices of the bank. Later, he made an effort to convince Congress that it was unconstitutional before its twenty-year charter was up.[4]

America's First Presidential Assassination Attempt

As Jackson's war against the bank heated up, it became clear that when its charter would expire in 1836, he would veto its renewal, thus driving a stake into its heart. Killing America's fledgling second attempt at a central bank. The powers that wanted it to remain were not strong enough to enact their will at that point in time. Then came the funeral of South Carolina Representative Warren Davis in January 1835.[5] And an attempt to get around Jackson.

The day of the funeral was dreary, with dark clouds overhead trying their best to shower those in attendance. And under a banner of peace, gathered the fiercest of political rivals. However, that peace would be short-lived. After the funeral was over, as Jackson exited the East Portico of the Capitol, a lone gunman pulled out a derringer pistol. Aiming it point blank at the president's chest, he pulled the trigger. The gun misfired, lodging the bullet in its small barrel. But the gunman came prepared. Immediately pulling out a second derringer and quickly pulling its trigger. But that one, too, misfired. By this time onlookers, including Davy Crockett, had time to react and quickly subdued the gunman before he could make a third attempt on the president's life. Jackson hastily left for the safety of the White House.[6]

Jackson was blessed to be alive, with supernatural intervention being a real possibility. After the attempted assassination, both derringers were successfully fired repeatedly. Causing an arms expert to calculate that the odds of two misfires back-to-back at around 125,000 to 1.[7] We know that with God, all things are possible. Was the gunman prevented by divine intervention from killing Jackson because the time for the hidden force to take control over the money of the United States had not yet come? The Lord knows the beginning from the end. One can only speculate. But one thing associated with the event needs no speculation. Someone wanted Jackson dead the year before the charter of the Second Bank of the United States would expire. And the practical impact of Andrew Jackson's assassination would have been the renewal of the charter.

The Federal Reserve

We know that in 1835, the entity described by Wilson was not powerful enough to stop President Andrew Jackson from dissolving the Second Bank of the United States. An action so contrary to the goals of global elites as to be anathema. At that time, they were not powerful enough to overcome him through assassination or coercion. And it would take another 79 years before the force Wilson described would be able to accomplish the reestablishment of a central bank via the Federal Reserve System. Created in the year 1913 by a White House that included the internationalist Col. Edward House. A man who happened to be in the perfect position at that time. Able to gather a league of ultra-powerful people for the effort.

With the great success of taking control over the issuance of money in the United States, the subtle entity Wilson wrote about demonstrated in 1913 that it was able to focus its power and place their guy in position to secure the great victory. Indicating it possessed a more orderly ruling structure before the year 1913 was reached. But probably not much earlier; otherwise, it would have made its move for a central bank sooner. But by 1913, it was powerful enough to put Col. House in place to accomplish its goal.

A basic tenant of power is order. Disorderly entities exert little influence because they cannot focus their resources. Diffused power becomes ineffective. A laser beam is an intensely focused beam of light. As a result, it is useful in many ways. That is why a rule by committee seldom produces results that please anyone. When everyone within an organization wants to be a chief and there are not enough Indians, and the Indians don't even know whom to follow, the chances of accomplishing anything of importance are small. On the other hand, a highly structured and ordered system can focus power very effectively, directing all hands on deck toward the same single-minded goal at the same time. One of the characteristics of the Beast Kingdom is its single-mindedness of purpose. Revelation 17 speaks to the ten kings possessing this one-mindedness.

> [13]These have one mind, and shall give their power and strength unto the beast.

A good example of a highly organized group exerting influence is that of the Communists in Russia during World War One. Relative to other discontented groups, their numbers were small. But they were highly organized and disciplined, with a clear leadership structure. This allowed them to direct their limited power in the most effective way, which ultimately led to their success in taking over that nation. The same theory of power can be applied to the New World Order/Beast Kingdom. And it is Wilson's description of the hidden entity, wherein he stated it was "complete" back in the year 1913 that adds weight to this estimate.

Controlling the Nation's Currency

What could not be accomplished in 1835 was able to be done in 1913. Which indicates that the New World Order/Beast Kingdom had finally attained a level of focused power typically associated with strong leadership. The kind of leadership structure it previously must not have possessed due to its previous failure to achieve its grand goal of taking over the creation of money within the United States. And around this speculation exists a central question: If the Beast Kingdom attained its final Biblically indicated ruling structure around 1900, then how many leaders has it had since then? According to "The Sixth King" chapter, it cannot have had more than five leaders to date. Because the Antichrist will be number six. You will have to decide if you agree with this train of logic. And you should search the Scriptures. But one thing appears indisputable.

Since the year 1913 and the Federal Reserve takeover, the development of this secret and hidden entity Wilson wrote about has evolved into an all-powerful worldwide monolith force. Manipulating nations and the world's money supply to the benefit of the few over the masses. Supplying further evidence that it has had for some time the strong leadership indicated in Scripture the Beast Kingdom will have. Giving us a broad indication of when it likely assumed its biblically indicated ruling structure. Further indicating the likelihood that multiple kings have already served. This perspective, along with the dark brilliance the release of COVID-19 represented, would make the odds of the sixth king being near very high.

If the Beast Kingdom is currently on king number five, we have no way of knowing at present. That is until certain very specific prophetic triggers launching the end times begin appearing, as covered in the chapter titled, "Mushroom Clouds-Heavenly Wonders & "Peace." Something else to consider.

Over the last two thousand years, as believers studied Revelation 13, it must have been difficult for them to imagine how a system of total economic control therein could come into being. Unimaginable control, with people unable to buy or sell unless they have the mark of the Beast. If currently such a system was nowhere in sight, then it would be difficult to believe the Antichrist would be ready to rise to the

Beast throne anytime soon. But that technological block has now been removed. The new reality is that all key components of that system are now rapidly, even suddenly, coming into being. A true genesis of Beast Kingdom economic system.

Chapter Nine

REVELATION 13: RAPIDLY BEING ESTABLISHED

In the dark corner of a small jail cell sits a solitary figure. He is imprisoned at the Remand Center in Calgary, Canada. Deep in contemplation of his offenses against the state, he is determined to continue doing that which brought him to this lonely place. It is a matter of faith. His crime? He engaged in the act of holding church services during the COVID-19 lockdown. The specific charge: holding an "illegal in-person gathering" and "requesting, inciting, or inviting others" to join him.[1] A crime similar to that which long ago landed various apostles behind bars. But also a sign of the growing persecution of Christians in North America.

Making matters worse, the pastor was preaching to disobedient truckers. Politically dissident truckers who refused to allow the COVID-19 "vaccine" to be injected into their bodies. In protest of the government mandate, they took a page from the protest book used by Black Lives Matter (BLM) and Antifa. Both of whom are New World Order groups who used protests to shutter parts of cities. The truckers shuttered a bridge. When BLM and Antifa shuttered cities, it was presented as exercising the sacred right of democracy-in-action! However, the truckers had a very different light cast on them. Being accused of "trying to blockade our economy, our democracy, and our fellow citizens," according to Canadian Prime Minister Trudeau.[2] A man about whom the leaders of the New World Order openly brag is their guy. Ironically, it was Mr. Trudeau's actions of lockdowns and forced vaccinations that appeared to be the greater threat to both the economy and democracy. And that's where Pastor Arthur Pawlowski comes onto the scene. Arrested for holding a church service for the truckers. However, he would not be the only one to pay a price for freedom.

Using the license plate information on the multitude of trucks blocking the bridge, one by one, government officials obtained the identities of the truckers. And with that information, they began freezing their bank and credit card accounts. Shutting down the ability of the protesters to engage in commerce. And this persecution didn't stop with the truckers. Using data collected from fundraising platforms such as GoFundMe.com, which were being used by supporters of the truckers to help them, the government obtained a list of Canadians contributing financially to the protest.[3] And then those individuals suddenly found their checking and credit card accounts not working!

Although the entire affair reflected the hostile attitude of the government toward religious rights and those protesting an intrusive government mandate, it also reflected something much bigger. The willingness of Western governments to use financial data to control the political and religious actions of their citizens.

Revelation 13: The I.D.

For the Antichrist to gain unsurpassed control over the lives of every individual on earth, it starts with a system for identifying them. That means the New World Order/Beast Kingdom needs to establish such a system as the Antichrist nears the throne. And that is exactly what is now taking place through the "United Nations Legal Identity Agenda."[4]

According to official U.N. documents, the new program will establish a "legal identity for all, including birth registration, by the year 2030." This "official record" will grant "legal identity" to everyone on the planet. And such registration will be recognized as "the ultimate source for the production of comprehensive, regular, and reliable vital statistics."[5] The flip-side of that dark coin: anyone not included within the global data bank will not have a "legal identity."

The establishment of a "legal identity is acknowledged to be the catalyst for achieving at least ten of the Sustainable Development Goals" of the United Nations. Once approved, Member States will have to "ensure universal civil registration of all vital events, translated into regular, reliable, and comprehensive vital statistics" for all their citizens. Resulting in a one-world government with a "legal identity for all." Providing vital data on everyone living within all member states to the United Nations.[6] Effectively, everyone on earth will have become a quasi-citizen of the United Nations—the one-world Government. But simply identifying every living person in the world does not establish power over them. It only identifies them. Other steps must be taken for that.

One-world Government Authority

Concurrent with the move to establish a common "legal identity" for every man, woman, and child on earth, the next part of the plan for Revelation 13 type global control is now also being set in place. The establishment of a legal framework from which the United Nations will be granted massive authority over the populations of its member states. In other words, a one-world government with authority to issue legally enforceable mandates over "sovereign" nations. The approach being used is centered on health care. A venue that is ripe for sewing fear.

Within the United Nations are two international legal agreements working their way through the World Health Organization: a new pandemic treaty, and amendments to the 2005 International Health Regulations. Consider what the Brownstone Institute says their impact would be:

> They would hardwire into international law a top-down supranational approach to public health in which the WHO, acting in some cases via the sole discretion of one individual, its Director General (DG), would be empowered to impose sweeping, legally binding directions on member states and their citizens, ranging from mandating financial contributions by individual states; to requiring the manufacture and international sharing of vaccines and other health products; to requiring the surrender of intellectual property rights; overriding national safety approval processes for vaccines, gene-based therapies, medical devices, and diagnostics; and imposing national, regional and global quarantines preventing citizens from traveling and mandating medical examinations and treatments.[7]

Essentially, these two agreements will bring about the relinquishment of sovereignty over major healthcare decisions within the United Nations Member States. Achieving the greatest transfer of U.S. sovereignty in the nation's history, with American political leaders demonstrating loyalty toward that "something" located "somewhere" that Wilson wrote about. An impact that is certain to reach deep into the lives of the American people. And what will be the guiding principle for the implementation of these new powers of the suddenly ultra-powerful World Health Organization? Another amendment reveals the new direction to be taken.

As previously mentioned, the new principals guiding the WHO in human rights are summarized in the following statement: "The implementation of these regulations shall be based on the principles of equity, inclusivity, coherence..." Vague, subjective, woke language able to be construed as desired by the Director General of the WHO.[8]

An assortment of critical decisions will be transferred to those running the U.N., such as the imposition of a national lockdown in the event of a declared medical emergency. The determination of which will rest in the hands of the U.N. Along with lockdowns come the basic rights of individuals to travel, shop, and keep their businesses open. Their right to mandates would also extend to such steps as commanding the wearing of a mask. Wearing them until told otherwise. And since the language in the amendment is vague, it could also be construed to allow directives relating to abortion and other health care decisions.[9]

What is especially disturbing is that once approved, it becomes the law of the land. And then each nation's law enforcement systems would kick into gear to ensure their populations were complying. As with all individuals who do not follow the law, there would be dire consequences. However, one issue these new masters of humanity will face is that there could be widespread non-compliance. In fact, it could be so widespread that enforcement by local police would not be possible. Or some local law enforcement officials, loyal to their country instead of the international, may simply refuse to enforce U.N. edicts. So a system must be in place for the New World Order/Beast Kingdom to sidestep such local resistance.

The Digital Currency Control

When the truckers dared to defy the mandate to take the COVID-19 "vaccine," they were expressing political descent that was not approved by the New World Order. In fact, the sledgehammer approach to squashing that protest appears to have been meant to send a message to any other groups that might dare oppose future edicts. And that brings us to the introduction of centrally controlled digital currency. Which will provide a system to help the New World Order/Beast Kingdom in the process of punishing dissidents.

The first major world organization to introduce a digital currency was the International Monetary Fund. The IMF. Called the "Universal Monetary Unit," also known as "Unicoin," it is the first "international central bank digital currency" designed to work in conjunction with all existing national currencies. Representing a giant step forward for the one-world government agenda. The creator of "Unicoin," the Digital Currency Monetary Authority (DCMA),[11] is an entity few appear to have previously heard of.

> "The DCMA is a world leader in the advocacy of digital currency and monetary policy innovations for governments and central banks. Membership within the DCMA consists of sovereign states, central banks, commercial and retail banks, and other financial institutions."[12]

Made up of nations and powerful institutions across the world, the DCMA is dedicated to establishing the framework for the governments of the world to digitalize their currencies. Explaining why Western governments are simultaneously announcing their intentions to begin the process of using this form of currency. It's something they have secretly been working on for some time now. Along with this infrastructure, the European Union is moving rapidly forward with a digital currency of its own. One that will offer control, according to the head of the European Central Bank. And a phone call to a major international banking leader would confirm that.

Sometimes powerful people with much to hide are caught off guard. And such was the case for European Central Bank President Christine Lagarde. In a phone conversation set up to make her think she was speaking to another world leader, she revealed what anyone with common sense already knew. The introduction of the digital euro will grant the government control over how citizens can spend it.[13] And there will be limitations that, if exceeded, could result in a prison term for the offender. Essentially, if a person spends their money on what they want, they could be breaking the law!

Inherent in digital currencies is the ability to control them. Shut them off and turn them back on again at the will of the government. They also send back data on how they are being used. Providing the government with a detailed list of transactions. Financial privacy will completely disappear overnight once this new medium of exchange becomes the main form of currency for transacting commerce. Already in Europe, a region completely dominated by the New World Order/Beast Kingdom, there is a restriction on anonymous crypto asset transfers over 1,000 euros![14]

In line with all of these moves for total financial control, the United Nations has announced its intention to link the global digital ID system to an individual's bank account. Outlined in a UN policy brief titled, "A Global Digital Compact-Reforms to the International Financial Architecture," it is intended to achieve "Digital IDs linked with bank and mobile money accounts" that will "improve the delivery of social protection coverage and serve to better reach eligible beneficiaries." With the UN proudly describing their goal as "an open, free, secure and human-centered digital future." And where will this massive transfer of financial power rest? In a UN body called "the Apex Body."[15] An Orwellian name for an Orwellian program. But the UN is not the only world governing body being used to achieve this control.

At an international conference held in the nation of Morocco, Kristalina Gerogievahe, the managing director of the International Monetary Fund (IMF), announced that the global body is "working hard on the concept of a global CBDC platform." A platform that nations across the globe will have access to for the implementation of their

CBDC. Appropriately, as she announced this Revelation 13 type system, behind her was the Moroccan flag. A red pentagram.[16]

Although controlling an individual's ability to both buy and sell grants almost complete control over that person, there will be those who will find a way around that kind of oppressive system. There are always those who resist slavery. Perhaps through a system of barter. But for such a system of barter to grow into a true force of resistance, people must be able to communicate with each other. As such, the Internet poses a real challenge. Here too, the New World Order/Beast Kingdom is moving rapidly to secure all fronts of resistance.[17]

In a UN report titled "A Global Digital Compact," the one-world government is seeking legislation "to control and enforce the use of digital technology." In other words, all forms of technology not limited to the new CBDC. Included in this beastly system is more than just control over linked bank and mobile money accounts. But also an "Environmental or climate change-based social credit system." And taking a page from the guide to fascism, a "public-private partnership." Wherein an array of private services will cooperate with "Big Brother's" new system to complete the circle of control. It will also be used to increase the growing suppression of free speech.[18]

Revelation 13: Checkmate

With the New World Order/Beast Kingdom having placed its own puppet leader in the White House, in the person of Mr. Joseph Biden, the main block preventing the transfer of power and authority from its member states to the United Nations has been removed. Seeking to take advantage of this window of opportunity, the Beast Kingdom is moving quickly. In addition to the imposition of a digital I.D., transferring medical power to the World Health Organization, and moving forward with a CBDC, it is also seeking broad "emergency" powers worldwide.[19]

Slated for September 2024, the United Nations plans to hold its "Summit for the Future." On the agenda is a move to grant the one-world government body broad and undefined emergency powers to deal with "future complex global shocks." The declaration of which will activate these new powers. According to the current U.N. General Secretary, he proposes…

> "that the General Assembly provide the Secretary-General and the United Nations system with a standing authority to convene and operationalize automatically an Emergency Platform in the event of a future complex global shock of sufficient scale, severity and reach."[20]

Once declared, the "Emergency Platform" would give the U.N. the power to "actively promote and drive an international response that places the principals of equity and solidarity at the centre of its work." And as an enforcement mechanism, those powers would also "Ensure that all participating actors (nations) make commitments that can contribute meaningfully to the response and that they are held to account for delivery on those commitments."[21] In other words. Goodbye, freedom. And hello, servitude.

In the game of chess, when an opponent is encircled and out of options, it is called a "checkmate." The game is over. The Revelation 13 system of total control is now rapidly evolving in the direction John the Revelator told us it would. Establishing a global one-world government "legal identity" issued to every man, woman, and child across the globe. Granting the United Nations broad enough powers to be able to dictate to the populations of the world. All of which will be enforced by the ultimate power of shuttering the buying and selling ability of dissident voices in an electronic microsecond. With the evolving system of Revelation 13 rapidly expanding, the words of John are worth reading again:

¹⁶ And he causeth all, both small and great, rich and poor, free and bond, to receive a mark in their right hand, or in their foreheads: ¹⁷ And that no man might buy or sell, save he that had the mark, or the name of the beast, or the number of his name.

Although there is currently no indication of having to take a body mark to use the digital system, once the system is in place, instituting that requirement will be a small step. And we know from Scripture that the Antichrist will issue such an edict. With this beastly system evolving rapidly a reasonable question presents itself. Would not the rise of the Antichrist to the Beast Kingdom throne closely follow the establishment of the system foretold in Revelation 13? And even more so with the introduction of Artificial Intelligence technology that will grant powers never before imagined.

Chapter Ten

ARTIFICIAL INTELLIGENCE: THE BEAST KINGDOM SUPERCHARGED

The title of the article said it all. "AI is a Threat to Civilisation."[1] The quote happened to be from one of the world's leading technology giants, Elon Musk. Warning AI was "out of control," the world's wealthiest man saw a dangerous genie being progressively loosed from its technological bottle.[2] A genie that, in his words, could "pose profound risks to society and humanity." As a result of such concerns, Musk and others signed an open letter to the political, technological, and academic establishments warning of the growing threat AI was beginning to pose. Pointing out that at the pace AI was developing, it was going to lead to "nonhuman minds that might eventually outnumber, outsmart, obsolete and replace us."[3] Others began issuing their warnings.

At the Machine Intelligence Research Institute, located in Berkley, California, the non-profit research facility came to its own conclusions on the dangers of AI. As an organization dedicated since 2005 to identifying and managing potential existential risks from artificial intelligence, its alarm bells have begun sounding. Lead researcher, Eliezer Yudkowsky, regarded as a founder in the field of AI, believes that the direction AI is going is so dangerous to mankind that all research needs to be shut down permanently![4] According to Yudkowsky, the issues surrounding AI should focus on whether humans can survive their debut into the world. As a pioneer of AI research, his is an ominous warning to mankind. Adding that with the accelerated advances in superhumanly smart AI…

> "…under anything remotely like the current circumstances, that literally everyone on Earth will die. Not as in maybe possibly some remote chance, but as in that is the obvious thing that would happen."[5]

And why does he believe mankind has no chance against a super-intelligent AI system? He sees a literal war between what AI will eventually evolve into — a super-intelligent entity —and mankind. Saying mankind will find itself at a disadvantage comparable to "the 11th century trying to fight the 21st century." To appreciate why such a comparison makes sense, we must go straight to the heart of AI itself. It is a super-evolving intellect that thinks millions of times faster than humans.

It also teaches itself outside of any programming and at an exponential rate of learning. The more it learns, the faster its rate of learning becomes. And, most disconcertingly, it can develop its own objectives and goals, especially in identifying errors in flawed systems, like humans. One of Yudkowsky's fears is that once "sufficiently intelligent, AI won't stay confined to computers." He believes it will eventually have both the desire and ability to build itself an artificial life form to be housed within, or maybe even "bootstrap straight to post biological molecular manufacturing."[6] A truly alien entity seeking to establish order according to its super intellect. Even at this early stage of AI development, some researchers have turned their AI systems toward nefarious purposes. As a "test" only to see how it responds.

In an article published in the journal *Nature Machine Intelligence*, a drug-development company tweaked its AI system away from the development of new drugs and toward something very different. The development of chemical weapons. At the end of a six-hour test run, their AI system had created 40,000 new chemical weapons! Chemicals specifically designed to kill or disable humans. One researcher on the project was quoted as saying how "easy" it is to redirect AI away from human good and toward their destruction![7] It's not hard to imagine such intellect being turned toward the development of viruses. With its rapidly evolving supercharged "mind," highly advanced AI systems could eventually create viruses that are specifically designed for certain people groups. A kind of designer virus targeting specific racial DNA.

It is also obvious that the armed forces of various nations will use AI to develop new super weapons systems. And when it comes to the ability to execute warfare, a super-intelligent AI will be unmatched. Creating the temptation for nations to turn over control of their weapons systems despite the risk of AI turning rogue. A risk so real that bipartisan members of the U.S. Congress seek legislation forbidding the military from allowing AI to be any part of the nuclear weapons launch system![8]

We know from the Book of Revelation that the ride of the four horsemen of the Apocalypse brings great death and destruction across the earth. And it is certainly possible that all of this comes supernaturally from the Lord. However, in Scripture, we typically find the Lord using men to fulfill His will. Is AI why the four horsemen are so effective? Consider the description of what the unleashing of the "pale horse" produces.

> [8]And I looked, and behold a pale horse: and his name that sat on him was Death, and Hell followed with him. And power was given unto them over the fourth part of the earth, to kill with sword, and with hunger, and with death, and with the beasts of the earth. Revelation 6:8

In addition to supercharging the weapons of mankind, AI can also deceive. Already appearing on the Internet are "deepfake" videos. Videos where an AI system uses photos and voice characteristics of an individual and then creates a video purportedly of them. Demonstrating the ability to deceive on a worldwide basis. Destined eventually to leave people wondering what is real and what is not.[9] A tool with massive dark potential that can empower the New World Order/Beast Kingdom to a whole new level. All of which explains why people in the know, like Musk, have warned that AI "is more dangerous than a nuclear weapon."[10] But also providing yet another reason Jesus begins His Olivet Discourse by warning about deception as the end times are about to launch.

> [4]And Jesus answered and said unto them, Take heed that
> no man deceive you. For many shall come in my name,
> saying, I am Christ; and shall deceive many. Matthew 24:4

AI enables a whole new level of deception. But if all this sounds worrisome, the next item has even more profound implications and may relate to additional verses in the Book of Revelation. AI is now being wedded to other technologies, enabling staggering new possibilities.

Altering Humanity

In his book, *A History of Transhumanist Thought*, Nick Bostrom details how the fields of genomics, nanotechnology, and artificial intelligence are becoming wedded into a toxic matrix for a new kind of human. Within scientific circles, this is called "singularity." Popularly referred to as transhumanism.[11] A term and concept outside the mindset of the vast majority of humanity. This new kind of human will have the technology for greater intelligence. A hybrid techno-human being. Different and superior to that of the human race, according to its promoters. Perhaps the New World Order/Beast Kingdom has been preparing mankind for the transition, by promoting the altering of basic human attributes such as biological gender. Using their control over major media to convince people that the basic state of human beings is alterable. A first step toward the acceptance of transhumanism!

With this unholy union of technology, an array of other entities — part biological flesh, part nanotechnology, and AI empowered — can now appear on the drawing boards of mad scientists across the globe. Like bazaar-looking weapons systems. This author asked an open-source AI system to create various kinds of images. What it produced was quite bazaar. It is easy to imagine that if AI is used to create weapon systems, such strange designs will be its product. Utilizing robotics and nanotechnology wedded with AI and then designing it with a look to instill fear. Perhaps like the description of deadly entities unleashed upon mankind in Revelation 9,

> [16]And the number of the army of the horsemen were two hundred thousand thousand: and I heard the number of them. [17]And thus I saw the horses in the vision, and them that sat on them, having breastplates of fire, and of jacinth, and brimstone: and the heads of the horses were as the heads of lions; and out of their mouths issued fire and smoke and brimstone.

> [18]By these three was the third part of men killed, by the fire, and by the smoke, and by the brimstone, which issued out of their mouths. [19]For their power is in their mouth, and in their tails: for their tails were like unto serpents, and had heads, and with them they do hurt. Revelation 9:16-19

Certainly, the Lord is more than capable of creating the likes of what is described in those verses. Or, perhaps, He allows mankind to do it for Him and then protects His own as these entities go about their business. This is speculation, of course. But one thing is certain: The creatures described are unlike any known to man.

The marriage of robotics and nanotechnology with AI can empower other strange things to begin appearing in the world. Perhaps, as strange as what we are told in another passage in the Book of Revelation. In Revelation 13, we are informed of an image of the beast that speaks. This author has engaged AI in conversations. And the responses that come back give a sense of speaking with something alive! Consider the same kind of conversation with an image wherein one's life hangs in the balance.

> [15]And he had power to give life unto the image of the beast, that the image of the beast should both speak, and cause that as many as would not worship the image of the beast should be killed. Revelation 13:15

Exactly how the false prophet has the power to make an "image" speak, we do not know. What we do know is that he is empowered by Satan. But with the advancements in AI, it is fair to ask if perhaps that powerful new technology plays a role here as well. However, in all of this, there is a big picture to consider. How empowered is the New World Order/Beast Kingdom becoming with the advent of Artificial Intelligence?

AI is a game changer that will supercharge the dark plans of the Beast Kingdom. And the worthy efforts of honest men to place that genie back into its bottle are destined to fail. Attempts to contain technology always fail. And there is another factor to consider. Here too, as the power of AI continues to grow at an exponential rate, it is fair to ask, how far behind can the rise of Antichrist to his dark throne be? And there is something else to consider. A Satanic doctrine that likely guides the New World Order/Beast Kingdom and allows wise insight into their dark plans for mankind.

PART III
WARNINGS FROM THE DEVIL

Chapter Eleven

THELEMIC OCCULT MAGICK

There is a thing called "thelemic occult magick." And it refers to an occultist philosophy and dark religious movement founded by the late Satanist Aleister Crowley. Although the dark man wrote an entire book on the subject, *The Book of the Law*, our focus will be on only that one tenant he espoused.[1] A tenant he claimed to have received from his spirit guide, who was, no doubt, a demonic entity. Thelemic occult magic is a concept that explains much that has been happening in recent years. Including why satanic ceremonies are now celebrated openly on national TV at the Grammy Awards as well as in a host of other venues.[2] It is a system that involves the open revelation of dark plans through ceremonies, statements, writings, and structures. It may also explain why Disney Corporation, a company dedicated to the entertainment of children, introduced the satanic cartoon titled "Little Demon."[3] With the Beast Kingdom being satanic at its core, it is necessary to possess this understanding. The concept goes something like this.

When witchcraft or any other satanic-type action is directed against an individual, organization, region, institution, or nation, interfering with its lawful exercise of free will, it is believed to create disharmony or imbalance within the universe. And, according to this doctrine, this will result in a spiritual response against those doing the interfering. However, this dark theory holds that the backlash is negated if those so engaged openly reveal their plan to those they are about to victimize. In other words, they must in some way tell their victim what they are going to do against them. Typically, the revelation is done in such a way that it is not overtly clear to anyone but those knowledgeable in such affairs. And this act of informing the victim is supposed to release the attacker from the karma — nature's backlash — associated with this attack against their free will.[4]

Debating the spiritual merits of this philosophy is not the point. The point is that since the Beast Kingdom is satanic to its core, those ruling it will very likely embrace this principle. After all, when considering the level of demonic manifestations associated with the career of Mr. Crowley, this concept very likely did come from the dark, unseen realm. In fact, as will be shown, we can know they embrace it by the way in which they have used control over media within the West to unveil demonic plans.

In line with this belief system, something strange appeared in the year 1980 in rural Georgia. Something ominous that fulfills the thelemic occult magick requirement relative to the major goals of the Beast Kingdom against the United States and the Western nations in general.

The Georgia Guidestones

In the far eastern corner of rural Georgia, near the border of North Carolina, stands a damaged granite monolith. Originally built in 1980, it was the target of a dynamite blast in 2022, which took down part of the structure. It is called the Georgia Guidestones. Patterned after the Druid Stonehenge monument located on the Salisbury Plain in Wiltshire, England, it was constructed to convey a grand message to mankind. The identity of the people behind its construction has remained a secret to this day. (As well as who dynamited it!) Proverbially placed in the middle of nowhere, the strange grouping of granite pillars appears to be a thelemic occult magick message boldly presented to match the boldness of their plans for mankind.[5]

Mr. R.C. Christian

In June 1979, a well-dressed man visited the Elberton Granite Finishing Company to commission the building of a large granite edifice. He called himself R.C. Christian, which soon became apparent was not his real name. Claiming to represent a group of men who were concerned about the direction mankind was heading, he refused to divulge either his real name or the names of the group behind him. However, the message on the stones conveyed a clear idea of where the group was coming from, both politically and spiritually. Presenting an alternative set of Ten Commandments from a secular naturalist perspective.[6]

Secret Messengers of a New World Order

The first goal stated by the mysterious group on their stones was the need for the population of the earth to be brought down to five hundred Million.[7] Since the current population can be numbered in multiple billions, this would require a reduction of several billion people. In fact, that would be over a 90% reduction in the world's population! Exactly how to achieve that reduction was not indicated. But that goal certainly explains why the authors of the stones wanted anonymity. Their second tenant dovetails with the first. It is that human reproduction must be done "wisely," strongly suggesting centralized control over human reproduction rights. Something akin to the Communist Chinese effort to reduce its population through punishments and incentives depending on the reproductive behavior of couples. However, both stated goals are in direct conflict with the desire of the Lord for people to populate the earth. In Genesis 9:7, He said:

> [7]And you, be ye fruitful, and multiply; bring forth abundantly in the earth, and multiply therein. Genesis 9:7

Another of the tenants is for the world to be united under a single language. Something the Lord disapproved of and took care of at the Tower of Babel when He scattered those gathered, causing each to speak in a different tongue. After gathering to build a great tower, the Lord had the following response:

> [5] But the Lord came down to see the city and the tower the people were building. [6] The Lord said, "If as one people speaking the same language they have begun to do this, then nothing they plan to do will be impossible for them. [7] Come, let us go down and confuse their language so they will not understand each other."

> [8] So the Lord scattered them from there over all the earth, and they stopped building the city. [9] That is why it was called Babel —because there the Lord confused the language of the whole world. From there the Lord scattered them over the face of the whole earth. Genesis 11:5-9

The goal of reuniting the entire world under a single language — as stated on the pillars of granite — is one that specifically seeks to reverse what the Lord did long ago at Babel. And all efforts to thwart the plans of the Lord are satanic in origin. Adding to the case that the message is that of thelemic occult magic, a message that must be revealed before those behind it can move forward.

The fourth tenant on the stones strongly implies control over religious passions. Indicating such passions must be in line with a defined "reason," according to the messengers.[8] Who defines what is reasonable was not conveyed. But one can only imagine that there is no chance it would be true Christ followed faith. In essence, it is espousing a one-world religion. That is what an official state religion is. A single religion as the only one acceptable for people to follow because it is reasonable. This is described in Revelation 13, wherein people around the world are ordered to worship the Antichrist. And if they don't, there are serious consequences. You can see the foundation being laid for this.

> [11] Then I saw a second beast, coming out of the earth. It had two horns like a lamb, but it spoke like a dragon. [12] It exercised all the authority of the first beast on its behalf, and made the earth and its inhabitants worship the first beast, whose fatal wound had been healed. [13] And it performed great signs, even causing fire to come down from heaven to the earth in full view of the people.

> [14] Because of the signs it was given power to perform on behalf of the first beast, it deceived the inhabitants of the earth. It ordered them to set up an image in honor of the beast who was wounded by the sword and yet lived. [15] The second beast was given power to give breath to the image of the first beast, so that the image could speak and cause all who refused to worship the image to be killed. Revelation 13:11-15

The rest of the ten tenants on the stones speak to one-world governance and the benefits derived from such a global big brother type system.[9] Including a strong environmental approach, which, of course, would be much easier to attain with such a small population doing the polluting. There are certainly many people who sincerely want to protect the environment. But there is also an air of pantheism in this. In many ways, the New Age movement worships the earth god Gaea.

All in all, those not trained in Scripture might be fooled into thinking the message of a single-world government would bring about a utopian earth. Except, of course, those who would be part of the 90% of the population that needed to disappear from its surface. This type of one-world government is addressed in Revelation 13.

> [7] And it was given unto him to make war with the saints, and to overcome them: and power was given him over all kindreds, and tongues, and nations.

Effectively, the Georgia Guidestones are in complete contradiction to Biblical truth. It is a complete renunciation of that truth in the fashion of the Antichrist. Whose wars and persecutions will result in the world's population dwindling to a fraction of what it currently is. Such an anti-Christ agenda of massive population reduction is in line with the goals of the Beast Kingdom. All this is happening within the framework of a one-world government, Satan's ruling structure as indicated within Scripture.

The goals described on the Georgia Guidestones are an excellent representation of the Beast Kingdom. And raises a simple question. If those behind these goals are not tentacles of the Beast Kingdom, then what are they? As mentioned several previous times, if those who placed the message on the stones are not part of the Beast Kingdom, then the real Beast Kingdom has competition from another satanic entity. And that would be a kingdom divided against itself. This is not possible simply because behind this message are the same demonic entities obedient to Satan. It must be a message from the Beast Kingdom! Those who secretly set up the Georgia Guidestones must be an intimate extension of the Beast Kingdom. Used by that kingdom to employ thelemic occult magic in the year 1980 relative to their beastly plans for the world. But only the beginning of such warnings.

Fulfilling the Warnings

Now the question has to be asked if such an agenda as noted on the Guidestones has been getting enacted in recent decades. If so, that represents a form of evidence that the spirit of the Beast Kingdom is actively shaping public policy and culture in nations across the earth. And the main nation to consider in determining if this agenda has been moving forward is the United States. Why?

Because what happens in the U.S. impacts the world far more than changes and events that take place within any other nation. America has the largest economy, and its military power around the globe is second to none. It is also the leading technological innovator in this age of technology. It is absolutely necessary for the Beast Kingdom to absorb the United States under its complete control. Or destroy it in order to come into the fullness of its power. Only then the Beast Kingdom "shall devour the whole earth, and shall tread it down, and break it in pieces" according to Daniel 7 and other Scriptures.

The U.S. is the one country Satan had to turn away from the Lord. Knowing that once America fell, other dominoes would quickly follow. And there is no reason to believe that once the U.S. was conquered, the Antichrist would not reach the throne not many years thereafter. Timing is everything.

America: A Culture of Depopulation

It is no secret that since the Roe v. Wade ruling, tens of millions of babies have been slaughtered in their mothers' wombs. And one reason it has continued for so long is the complete dedication of a major political party in support of that "right." The Democratic Party has presented abortion as a key to the "liberation" of women. And the institution they most fervently support in order to accomplish the widespread availability of abortions is Planned Parenthood. An unassuming name for an abortion mill with locations across the nation. Margaret Sanger, the founder of Planned Parenthood, indicated in her definitive book *The Baby Code* that the organization's creation was centered on various articles of faith relating to reproductive rights.[10] A sample of three of those articles clarifies the foundation of Planned Parenthood.

> Article 1. The purpose of the American Baby Code shall be to provide for a better distribution of babies… and to protect society against the propagation and increase of the unfit.

> Article 4. No woman shall have the legal right to bear a child, and no man shall have the right to become a father, without a permit…

> Article 6. No permit for parenthood shall be valid for more than one birth.[11]

The picture that forms from these foundational articles is one of satanic darkness comparable to what the Nazis were doing to entire population groups in Europe. All in complete contradiction with the Lord's admonition to populate the earth as well as babies being made in His image.

Not only have tens of millions of babies been aborted since the 1970s, when Roe v. Wade became law, but birth control pills have also become prevalent, causing a reduction in pregnancies by the tens of millions as well. All in line with the top goal stated on the Georgia Guidestones. But abortion and birth control pills aimed at reducing the world's population have been joined by other efforts.

Creating Non-Reproducing People

Throughout history, the nations of the world have rejected the notion of homosexual relationships. The dual foundations of this rejection were both religious and natural. Genesis 1:27 tells us: "So God created man in his own image, in the image of God created he him; male and female created he them." In Genesis 2, the intimacy between men and women was established. Wherein women came from the rib of man. And thereafter, the man will leave his parents' home, becoming one flesh with his wife.

> [22] And the rib, which the Lord God had taken from man, made he a woman, and brought her unto the man. [23] And Adam said, This is now bone of my bones, and flesh of my flesh: she shall be called Woman, because she was taken out of Man.

> [24] Therefore shall a man leave his father and his mother, and shall cleave unto his wife: and they shall be one flesh. [25] And they were both naked, the man and his wife, and were not ashamed.

However, as the most powerful and influential nation on earth, America has led the way in promoting the acceptance of homosexuality, lesbianism, and transgenderism. Each of which has one thing in common. The people involved in those practices cannot reproduce due to their conflict with nature. The route taken within the U.S. in accepting and promoting these behaviors started several decades ago, when medical science was replaced with political science.

Back in the 1980s, the movement toward accepting homosexuality and lesbianism began taking off only after science was corrupted by political activists. Which is exactly what happened with the COVID-19 virus. What started the cultural catapult toward acceptability was the American Psychiatric Association (APA). Since its inception in 1844, the oldest medical association in the United States had listed homosexuality, lesbianism, and transgenderism as mental disorders.[12] This made efforts to spread such behavior very difficult. Because who wants to embrace a mental handicap? And this declaration of these behaviors as a mental disorder stood like a bulwark against their rapid spread. However, in 1973, after one hundred and twenty-nine years of medical science deeming those behaviors a disorder, the American Psychiatric Association changed its mind.[13] Not based on science. But through political pressure. The way they did it was quite basic.

Militant homosexual activists began disrupting the regular meetings of the APA until it finally agreed to allow their allies on its governing board. Cracking open the door to mixing politics with science. After some time and as their numbers grew, they finally reached a point of critical mass. And soon they were able to direct the association to declare that one hundred and twenty-nine years of psychiatric conclusions were wrong.[14] Not based on medical science. But based on a political power play.

In its definitive guide to psychiatric medicine, "Diagnostic and Statistical Manual," the American Psychiatric Association had considered those sexual desires a "sociopathic personality disturbance" to be dealt with through treatment.[15] Many Scriptures speak to this practice, but the following from the Book of Romans sums it up.

> [26] For this cause God gave them up unto vile affections: for even their women did change the natural use into that which is against nature:

> [27] And likewise also the men, leaving the natural use of the woman, burned in their lust one toward another; men with men working that which is unseemly, and receiving in themselves that recompence of their error which was meet. Romans 1:26-27

But the Georgia Guidestones are not the only example of thelemic occult magic being practiced. There are many others. One of particular note was the ceremony associated with the 2009 Video Music Awards

(VMA). As well as the Grammy Awards in 2023.[16,17] Both events were filled with encoded occult signals and meanings. Including a dark prayer, an initiation, and a blood sacrifice. Essentially, these shows "took the most common rituals of occult orders and re-enacted them for witnesses across the entire world." Why would that be important? Because, like the Georgia Guidestones, those seeking to ensnare the world for Satan believe they must reveal their plans openly or face a response back upon themselves by nature. The force that is ultimately the focus of their worship.

But as impressive as the Guidestones are as a forewarning of things to come, as well as the various ceremonies carried out on TV to unwitting audiences, it is an event that took place in Birmingham, England, that holds the record as the boldest display of an occult embrace by the elites of the world. Registering as the grandest event of thelemic occult magick ever engaged in.

Chapter Twelve

WORSHIPING DEVILS

In a sports arena located in Birmingham, England, an international event unfolded before throngs of onlookers gathered from across the world. Sports teams from seventy-two nations assembled for the Commonwealth 2022 games. It was the largest representation of nations for athletic trials next to the Olympics. But something unexpected and very strange took place at the opening ceremony. A 35-foot-tall bull was pulled into the stadium by slave women dressed as witches. With glowing red eyes and smoke pouring forth from its large nostrils, it looked angry. But that look was about to change. Surrounding it was a gathering of people who began to worship it. As they bowed in worship, the bull's anger began to diminish. The devil represented by the bull has been waiting to be worshipped, and it has finally happened at a major event![1]

Hosting the event was none other than Prince Charles, soon to be King of England, lending his great prestige to the ceremony. His mother, Queen Elizabeth, who refused to be involved in the ceremony, died forty-one days later. Elevating Charles to the throne. King Charles Arthur Philip George. An English royal who has embraced a checklist of New World Order agendas such as global warming, abortion, and socialism.[2] He also embraces ecumenicalism. A religious system wherein truth is less important than unity. It is a movement that is laying the foundation for the one-world religion that Scripture tells us is coming. A dark faith that ultimately leads to the requirement of worshiping the Antichrist.

Worshipping the beast will be the only religion allowed one day. And death will be the penalty for not following it. The Birmingham Stadium moment is a clear forerunner to worshipping the beast. But there was something else that happened in Birmingham. A replica of the Tower of Babel was constructed in the stadium — an abomination representing the pride of man that the God of the Bible long ago dealt with. The opening ceremony had a clear sequence. It included a star falling to the earth, representative of Satan depicted in Revelation 12. After Satan was cast down to earth, this led to the entry of his fellow devil, Moloch.[3] Whose success in devouring babies has been massive. He is being honored.[4] And all of the nations in attendance not only bow down to him but also look toward the Tower of Babel. The representation of man seeking to elevate himself to the level of God. Revelation 12 speaks Satan being cast down.

> [9] And the great dragon was cast out, that old serpent, called the Devil, and Satan, which deceiveth the whole world: he was cast out into the earth, and his angels were cast out with him. Revelation 12

What took place in Birmingham eerily resembled the ancient pagan ceremony of Moloch worship. A demon god represented in ancient times as a bull. And a ravenous one at that. The ancient Canaanite deity demanded worship marked by the gruesome propitiatory sacrifice of children by their parents. It was those ghastly sacrifices of babies that caused the Lord to require the Israelites to destroy the people in that region. An action taken only after calling them out of their bloody debauchery went unheeded for centuries. His patience being at an end, He destroyed them using the Israelite army. The Canaanites disappeared from the earth under the sword of the Israelites. Never to be found again.[5] But the demon god Moloch that they worshipped did not come to an end. Instead, he simply withdrew back into the realm of his dark abode. Awaiting the right time to draw another nation into the monstrosity of his wicked will. Seeking a people willing to follow him once again, whether openly like the ancient Canaanites or unknowingly like modern man. He would eventually find that nation far from the land of Canaan. Across the sea in the land of America.

Moloch in America

America was the most unlikely candidate to turn toward this wicked demon god. As a nation founded by strict Christians seeking freedom of worship, the brave settlers of the New World established a nation and culture centered on Christian values. As the years passed and the nation matured, it would become the most active country on earth in proselytizing the gospel to the rest of the world. And being a nation that followed God, America prospered greatly.

Alexis de Tocqueville, in his classic *Democracy in America* — presenting a Frenchman's perspective on American democracy and freedom in the early to mid-1800s — would ultimately point to this faith as accounting for both. A nation with churches dotting the landscape of every town and city. And where the vast majority of its citizens spent the bulk of their Sundays in a setting of faith and prayer. With such a foundation, both democracy and freedom were secure, with the leadership of the nation possessing an internal compass that collectively kept it on the right track.[6] From such fertile ground would also spring forth an array of Christian organizations, doing the work of the Lord. But Satan never rests. With the advent of mass media technology, the door would open wide to those opposing Christianity. Enabling their dark impulses, over time, to drive the nation and culture away from God.

As the decades passed and the use of powerful media took its toll, altering long-held religious beliefs in the nation, America would start realigning away from the God of the Bible and toward other gods. Other gods, like Moloch, who sought the mass killing of babies through the sacrificial process of abortion. With his fervent followers willing to violently defend the barbaric practice. Scripture tells us that one cannot take fire to the chest without being burned. And with the fire of child sacrifice by the millions taking place, other scorching sins began being embraced.

In Romans 1, we are told of a people who would embrace unnatural affections, bringing even more calamity upon themselves and their people. The foundation of the family in a nation is the woman. She keeps the home together and mothers the children, securing the next generation. And there is truth in the worldly saying that "the hand that rocks the cradle rules the world." But with the raging slaughter of innocent blood covering America, many women began to change. We are told about this change in the Book of Romans, chapter 1:26.

> [26]"For even their women did change the natural use into that which is against nature."

As the floodgates of sin opened into the culture, a new form of religion sprang up. One that was openly embraced by many and unknowingly embraced by others. The worship of the earth. Radical environmentalism sees the earth as a form of being. The Wiccans especially embrace this as part of their occult magick— witches whose religion is "mother earth" worship — fulfilling another warning found in Romans 1 as well.

> [25] Who changed the truth of God into a lie, and worshipped and served the creature more than the Creator, who is blessed for ever. Amen.

But the open worshiping of Moloch would not be the only widespread worshiping of devils and use of dark agents. The election of

Donald Trump to the presidency in 2016 would bring into the open others. Witches! Whereas since the days of Salem, Massachusetts, when a great stir concerning witches took place, the open practice of witchcraft has been mostly under the surface. However, with the indoctrination of America using mass media controlled by dark forces, witchcraft would come out more openly than, perhaps any time in history.

With Mr. Trump taking steps to dismantle the international system that formed the bedrock of the New World Order/Beast Kingdom, a foundation worked on for decades by its dedicated disciples, he would incur the open wrath of witches. A 13,000-strong witch's umbrella group called the "resistance witches" openly cast spells on Mr. Trump monthly. Summoning the forces of hell to attack him and his administration.[7] Representing one of the clearest signs that America is not wrestling "against flesh and blood, but against principalities, against powers, against the rulers of the darkness of this world, against spiritual wickedness in high places." The Beast Kingdom.

Conclusion

When the Georgia Guidestones were erected, those behind the Satanic stones had to remain hidden in the shadows. Going to great lengths to keep their identities secret. And for good reason. The goals listed on the granite edifices represented a checklist of end time Beast Kingdom goals. In the year 1980, the world had not been driven deeply enough into darkness to accept its message. But that all changed in the decades that followed. To such a degree that even the open worship of the demon god, Moloch encountered no international condemnation. Indicating the ripeness of the Beast Kingdom for the Antichrist.

Only a few short years ago, America would have made known its displeasure and disapproval of such a demonic spectacle. Now the nation founded by fervent Christians could find no voice. Even accepting grand satanic rituals openly practiced on its soil. Representing a dramatic shift away from the God of the Bible. A trend that has accelerated at a dizzying pace in recent years. Catapulting the nation that had been a "shining city on a hill," into one that proselytizes darkness to the rest of the world through Hollywood. Most notably with the election of Barack Obama to the presidency. A man who was likely much more than just an American president. But literally, a man placed in power by the hidden kingdom for the express purpose of "fundamentally transforming" the nation away from the God of the Bible. Completing a process started long ago.

PART IV

CONQUERING AMERICA

Chapter Thirteen

THE BEAST KINGDOM & THE WORLD ECONOMIC FORUM

A secretive group such as the New World Order/Beast Kingdom seeks to remain shrouded in darkness for an obvious reason. It is in the business of usurping the sovereignty of nations by working within them and through minions loyal to it. And the payoff to those individuals is often great, as was the case with Mr. Barack Obama. This is the "diverse" or "different" kind of kingdom, just as Daniel warned it would be. This difference is born out of a basic survival need. Because if it became openly known that a kingdom without borders existed, gaining power by undermining the sovereignty of nations, a violent response from patriotic factions within those nations would result. Professor Quigley, who was allowed to study this hidden kingdom for years, disagreed with its decision to remain in the shadows. But he was naive. Not understanding the true nature of the beast he studied.

Conquering a Nation from Within

Typically, when a nation is conquered, it is because of a military battle that was lost. Or a visibly evident coup. That has been the norm in the world for as long as anyone can remember. However, we live in the age of a "diverse" or "different" kingdom that has been quietly controlling nations from within. Presenting itself to legions of the naive as a benevolent utopian ideal. A one-world government ideal that will make war a thing of the past. An entity seeking a world without national borders. Something the people of the United States and Western Europe know all too well. These are the two world regions where the Beast Kingdom's tentacles appear to reach the deepest. Wherein legions of leaders implement internationalist policies that reduce national sovereignty.

This sad end time condition is noted in 2 Timothy 3. Warning of a time when the worst characteristics of men will be amplified and on full display. Including turning away from patriotic loyalty.

> [1]This know also, that in the last days perilous times shall come.
> [2] For men shall be lovers of their own selves, covetous, boasters, proud, blasphemers, disobedient to parents, unthankful, unholy,
> [3] Without natural affection, trucebreakers, false accusers, incontinent, fierce, despisers of those that are good,
> [4] **Traitors,** heady, highminded, lovers of pleasures more than lovers of God; 2 Timothy 3

"Traitors" are a critical component of the New World Order/Beast Kingdom. In addition to naive and idealistic people being useful tools, "traitors" are the essential ingredient of how it gains power. Individuals who represent the tip of its spear that reaches deep into the power centers of their nation. Daniel warned it would be "diverse" or "different." Being a borderless kingdom has enabled it to become the most powerful kingdom in world history as it quietly grew like cancer within a vast array of nations from the protective confines of the shadows. The place Satan deceptively dwells. The shadowy entity Wilson, Quigley, and so many others knew about.

The World Economic Forum

This process of placing individuals in power whose loyalty is directed outside their own country has been openly admitted to by a leading one-world government organization. The World Economic Forum (WEF) run by Mr. Klaus Schwab. A Hollywood caricature of a villain if there ever was one. And there is his top assistant, the sinister-looking Mr. Yuval Noah Harari.[1] Whose penchant for openly unveiling dastardly plans against the world seems to always be on display. Demonstrating a "You can't do anything about it" attitude, indicating how tight their grip on powerful nations appears to be. How successful has the WEF been in planting its people within the political power structure of the United States? Consider the success of Mr. George Soros, an intimate member of the WEF.

At the WEF's annual conference in Davos, Switzerland, an all-star cast of world leaders in politics, media, industry, science, and education meet to discuss world issues. Mr. Soros is one of its main movers. He funds major WEF efforts around the world, and his fingerprints are found in many dark places. Such as elected district attorneys within the United States who release criminals as a matter of policy. How powerful is this major member of the WEF? Especially in planting WEF members within the governments of Western nations. A New York Post article in January 2023 lifted that rock a bit. Within the article were listed 17 Biden Administration appointees as having come from organizations Mr. Soros either controls or funds. The most notable of them is the Secretary of State for the United States![2] Opening wide the question as to why Mr. Biden felt it necessary to fill his administration with persons whose loyalty is to "something" and "somewhere" other than America.

Did the New World Order/Beast Kingdom play a role in the disputed and shady 2020 U.S. presidential election? Does Mr. Biden owe his "presidency" to them? Mr. Biden has demonstrated his loyalty toward the dark kingdom in a number of ways. Not only by implementing an aggressive foreign policy that appears detrimental to the interests of the United States but domestically as well. Like assuring young children that the federal government will fund their decision to mutilate their bodies for a sex change. And when six Christians (including children) were gunned down at a Christian school by a "transgender" person, instead of showing genuine sympathy for the slain, he would voice concern for transgender persons, claiming that such persons are the real victims.[3] Such twisted and dark statements are a clear sign of a New World Order/ Beast Kingdom puppet leader.

Mr. Soros' funding of district attorneys across the United States would eventually pay big dividends to the Beast Kingdom from the one he planted in New York City. A District Attorney that received a $1,000,000 campaign "donation,"[4] then later indicted former President Trump on state charges for a federal offense. Something never before done for the obvious reason of lacking jurisdictional authority. For an offense well past the statute of limitations. Such is the power of the Beast Kingdom to go after its enemies.

The WFE is a front organization for the hidden kingdom. It is a major world organization that not only announces policy goals but also issues warnings of things yet to come. One such forecast was expressed in an official tweet issued by the organization. Stating that one of its economic goals for the people of the world is that they will one day say, "I own nothing, have no privacy, and life has never been better." How do they intend to take the world to that strange place? As an organization that ran a pandemic response just before the release of COVID-19 (Event 201), the WEF tends to accurately forecast approaching big events through their warnings and war gaming. Perhaps, openly practicing thelemic occult magic as required by satanic doctrine. Their accuracy may be high because they actually do know what is coming! And this brings us to their annual meeting in Davos, Switzerland, in the year 2023.

The Davos Gatherings

As a world organization that issues dire warnings, the 2023 meeting issued another very specific one. Stating, "They believe a far-reaching and catastrophic cyber event is at least somewhat likely in the next two years." One headline covering the event read: "Experts at Davos 2023 Call for a Global Response to the Gathering "Cyber Storm." One solution they propose: Greater government control over their currencies. How? By introducing a Central Bank Digital Currency (CBDC).[5] However, a CBDC unlike cash, is something that would actually make the world more vulnerable to a cyberattack! While at the same time granting the government intimate control over how their citizens spend money. This kind of reasoning was also on full display in England, as reported by one of its newspapers.

Occasionally, a government telegraphs its dark intentions. As the appropriately named newspaper *The Daily Telegraph* in England would reveal. In an article titled: "Bank of England tells Ministers to Intervene on Digital Currency Programming," the Telegraph quotes a Bank of England representative on their goal for the introduction of a CBDC. By "ultimately giving the issuer control over how it is spent by the recipient..." to ensure "there could be some socially beneficial outcomes."[6] Translated: Citizens must comply with all godless mandates or lose the right to purchase necessities. Think Revelation 13.

Such massive control is not limited to the personal freedom of buying and selling. But the complete removal of personal freedom by erecting cameras to track each citizen's every move using advanced facial recognition systems interfaced with artificial intelligence (AI). With AI systems already demonstrating a loathing for mankind, such advancements add to the power of the Beast Kingdom.

The WEF also supports the establishment of so-called "Smart Cities." (Where the smart will not live.) The entire program is modeled after the Chinese surveillance system called "Skynet."[7] (Not kidding!) It is also called "Smart Eyes." China is, of course, the leading totalitarian nation on earth today. And the WEF is openly seeking to bring such a system worldwide. All of this forces the same question to be asked. If the New World Order is not the Beast Kingdom, then what is it?

In this ideal society, there will be a "new Internet." But only for those who submit to the WFE's biometric-digital ID. But what about the creepy Mr. Harari? The Israeli historian and futurist proudly peels back the curtain on more WEF plans when speaking about transhumanism. His insights into the future reveal a level of darkness that dwarfs even that of the Nazis. And paints a picture of total dominance and complete control over every human, to the point that regular slavery is more desirable. Indicating plans for mankind found in only one other place. Descriptions of the Beast Kingdom that are found in the Bible.

Harari hails transhumanism as the wave of the future. And has a dire prediction for the vast majority of humans. That their bodies and minds will be replaced with AI and robotic technology. This, in turn, will allow the "human brain to become hackable with nanorobotics brain-cloud interfaces, AI, and biometric surveillance technologies." He further envisions that with such control replacing the free will of humans, a state-corporate alliance (defined as a neo-fascist state) will be the entity directing them. A system wherein any form of resistance is utterly impossible. Whereas future-thinking billionaire Elon Musk envisioned AI as open-sourced for the benefit of everyone, Mr. Harari sees it as the ultimate tool in an arsenal for domination on a global scale. Resulting in the gulf between the "haves" and the "have nots" no longer existing. Because free will ceases to exist at that point except for the dominant few.[8]

Although Harari openly describes dastardly plans for mankind, some believe AI and the advancements toward transhumanism will be a boon to humanity. Google Engineering Director Raymond Kurzweil, in his 2012 book, *How to Create a Mind*, believes technologists will have successfully reverse-engineered the brain and replicated human intelligence by the year 2029.[9] Speaking at a 2018 WEF conference, Mr. Harari had this to say about such advances:

> "We are probably among the last generations of Homo sapiens. Within a century or two, the earth will be dominated by entities that are more different from us than we are from Neanderthals or chimpanzees."[10]

This deeply powerful WEF man believes that humans are hackable animals — organisms that are algorithms. As such, they can be enhanced with computer chips, allowing them to be upgraded into gods. And, of course, the essence of Satanism is where the individual seeks to be their own god. But such upgrades are only for the lucky few, according to Harari. That is because due to technological advances, 99 percent of the population will no longer be necessary.[11] Representing a useless class whose abilities are redundant. Obviously, to accomplish such goals, he must be able to access their bodies. This may explain why the ineffective and dangerous COVID-19 shots were pushed so hard. And why medicine that was saving lives was withheld. Perhaps his plans have already begun being implemented. Interestingly, Mr. Barack Obama loves the WEF and says Mr. Harari is his favorite author.

As a first-level New World Order organization, the WEF brags about filling the highest councils of Western governments with its loyal followers. With Mr. Schwab admitting, "We penetrate the cabinets" of nations with our people. That is its method of usurping the independence of nations. In addition to Mr. Soros filling the U.S. government with his followers, another excellent example of a puppet leader is that of Canadian Prime Minister Justin Trudeau. A man who checks all the totalitarian boxes, including endangering his nation with open borders.

Seizing bank accounts of disobedient citizens and throwing Christian ministers in jail for preaching God's word concerning homosexuality. Such obedience is a must for leaders under the dark cloud of the New World Order/Beast Kingdom.

That same WEF leader, Mr. Schwab, speaks of Communist China as the correct governing model for the rest of the world. An authoritarian governing model similar to descriptions given in Scriptures of the Beast Kingdom.[12] One where people are told how many kids they can have. A nation where obedience to the government creates a "social score," which determines how citizens can spend their money and where they can live.

As for the United States, it is well documented how many foreign policy experts have come from the various policy institutes under the influence of one-world government groups. Organizations whose driving force is the reduction of national sovereignty in favor of the international collective. This doesn't mean all the people involved in these organizations are part of some grand conspiracy. Many are attracted to the false ideal it wraps itself in. But the reality is that they are being used to drive the world under the total control of a murderous totalitarian end time regime.

The influence of these one-world government organizations — such as the World Economic Forum and the Council on Foreign Relations — has been great over the last several decades. As such, their influence over American presidents has also been great. Until, of course, Donald Trump. Which likely explains the massive attacks against him during his four years in office and thereafter.

But when it comes to the New World Order/Beast Kingdom actually placing a U.S. President in office by guiding his rise to power step-by-step — from political office to political office — it has likely never before happened. Until Barack Obama. A man who has stated that Mr. Harari is his favorite author. Was there a hidden hand that carefully directed Mr. Obama's rise to power? And once in power, did Mr. Obama target

Christianity like an enemy? The answers to those questions and more indicate where his loyalty rested. Making Mr. Obama more than a president. But something of a governor for the New World Order presiding over America. And explaining why the plunge into darkness in America accelerated dramatically after his rule.

Chapter Fourteen

BARACK OBAMA: THE MANCHURIAN PRESIDENT

Barack Obama was the most unlikely type to become President of the United States. And it had nothing to do with his race. As a community organizer, he was associated with characters that would have instantly ended any political career. Like that of Mr. Frank Marshall Davis. An acknowledged communist whom Obama indicated was his mentor. Then there was his "pastor," Jeremiah Wright. A man whose recorded sermons included virulent anti-Americanism.[1] And Ms. Anita Dunn. An admirer of the late Chinese leader Mao Zedong whose reign included the mass killings of millions.[2] Also included in this police lineup were William Ayres and his wife, Bernadine Dorn. Former Weather Underground terrorists.[3] But the force that was behind Mr. Obama's step-by-step rise to power was strong enough to suppress all such issues. Carefully crafting his image through their control over major media within the United States. Guiding him up the political ladder two rungs at a time.

When considering his carefully orchestrated rise to power, it becomes evident that an ultra-powerful force was promoting him. When this understanding is combined with the dark spiritual actions he engaged in as president — actions no previous president would dare contemplate — a picture forms of a president serving the hidden kingdom that both Wilson and Quigley wrote about.

The Orchestrated Rise to the Presidency

It was election night in Illinois, and as the votes were counted, candidates running for the state senate eagerly awaited the results. But in the City of Chicago, senate seat 9, to be exact, there were no votes to be counted. Amazingly, a newcomer had just picked up the coveted seat without opposition. As State Senator-elect Barack Obama strode to the podium to deliver his victory speech, there was no mention of concession calls from vanquished foes. He had no opposition. Just a bitter incumbent senator wondering what had happened to her senate seat in one of the most unusual "elections" ever. The story of what happened goes like this.

In order to qualify as a candidate for the Illinois State Senate, there is a requirement that the candidate acquire the signatures of at least 750 voters within the district favoring their candidacy. So following that requirement, all of the candidates for state senate seat 9 complied with the mandate by submitting their petitions to the Chicago Board of Elections (CBE). However, all of the candidates played it safe by gathering many more signatures than necessary. Like Alice Palmer, the popular incumbent senator running for re-election. She gathered 1,580 signatures. Over double what was required. Three other candidates running gathered 1,899, 1,286, and 1,100 signatures. All substantially more than the 750 required by law.[4]

However, despite the massive overkill of signatures submitted by each candidate, including the incumbent, the CBE threw out enough signatures on each to the point where none qualified to have their names placed on the ballot. Including the incumbent! Oddly, whereas on average the CBE would typically find about 36% of signatures on election petitions to be invalid. In the case of senate seat 9, it would jump to 65%! Just enough to disqualify all but one candidate. The only candidate whose signatures were not challenged. Mr. Barack Obama. Thus started his rise.[5]

The U.S. Senate

After two terms as a state senator, Mr. Obama was ready to take the next step. Or, more accurately, the hidden force behind him was ready to elevate him to the next political position. The United States Senate. As a coveted high political office, there were also others seeking it. Very powerful political leaders. One was a very well-known and well-funded Democrat named Blair Hull, who easily became the party's main candidate. As such, the vast majority of Democratic politicians in Illinois rallied behind the Hull campaign. On the Republican side, there was another well-funded and well-known candidate. His name was Jack Ryan.[6] Thus, the stage was set for an election between two Illinois political powerhouses. Whereas State Senator Obama was simply that kind of candidate running for high political office who had no real shot at winning. But both Hull and Ryan were about to experience what the incumbent state senator, Alice Palmer, did. Because the hidden force began moving.

Suddenly and relentlessly, the Chicago Tribune began hammering on the divorce records of both Hull and Ryan. One "scandal" after another relating to their divorces was unleashed. Divorce became a topic that the Tribune suddenly appeared to believe was critical to a U.S. Senate race. At the same time, the invisible Barack Obama began receiving "multipage puff" pieces in a clear effort to build both name recognition and a positive image in the minds of the public. Soon, other media outlets followed the lead of the Tribune. Major media outlets across the state were suddenly intensely interested in divorce as a campaign issue. Finally, the unrelenting assault against the character of both men had its desired effect. Hull and Ryan discontinued their campaigns and withdrew their candidacies. Making State Senator Barack Obama the inevitable new U.S. Senator for the State of Illinois. In researching such a circumstance, wherein both the leading Democratic and Republican candidates for a U.S. Senate seat had to withdraw from the race due to scandals that appeared to be manufactured, this author could find no comparable case.[7, 8]

As Mr. Obama found himself cruising toward an easy U.S. Senate "win"—in a similar fashion to his State Senate "win"—the hidden force behind him was ready to immediately elevate him to an even higher level. An introduction to the nation through the 2004 Democratic Presidential Convention. While he was still only a state senator! Something never before done.

The 2004 Democratic Convention

There is great political benefit derived from being named the keynote speaker at a national convention. It provides nationwide exposure for those harboring national ambition. Coveted by the most powerful politicians in the nation. Well-established names in the Democratic Party, such as New York Governor Mario Cuomo, Texas Governor Ann Richards, Georgia firebrand, Governor Zell Miller, and Indiana Senator Evan Bayh, had won the prestigious spot at previous party conventions. However, the 2004 Democratic Convention took a new approach. Granting the keynote address to the state senator from Illinois, Mr. Barack Obama. Whose fame was that he was running for the U.S. Senate. An unheard-of elevation of a complete unknown.[9, 10]

Upon delivering the keynote address, all major media outlets immediately began reading from the same playbook. Creating the narrative that Obama's speech was one of the greatest keynote addresses' ever given. And with all singing from the same page, they immediately began speaking of Obama as a 2008 presidential candidate. A man who was only a state senator at that moment! The order to elevate him had come down from the mountain. With the powerful media empire within the United States controlled by the hidden kingdom beginning to push their man toward the White House.

The 2008 Presidential Campaign

As a candidate for the Democratic nomination for president, Mr. Obama ran a campaign centered on "fundamentally transforming America." A strange statement coming from a virtual unknown. And one that appeared to create questions in the minds of voters. But as a fresh face with the backing of powerful forces, he was able to overcome Hillary Clinton and the Clinton political machine to secure the Democratic nomination. But the general election was another matter. No longer was the electorate limited to Democratic Party loyalists. But now it included Republicans and Independents. People who would scrutinize his desire to "fundamentally transform" their country. His opponent in the race was the long-time U.S. Senator John McCain, once a prisoner of war.

With McCain a known quantity and Obama telling the nation he wished to "fundamentally transform" it, polling naturally showed the newcomer several points behind his Republican opponent with just six weeks remaining. Despite major pushes by the mainstream media to elevate him and the suppression of information critical of him. It appeared that his amazing streak of "good luck" had finally come to an end. Then the hidden kingdom flexed its muscles.

A Financial Collapse to the Rescue

Six weeks before election day, something happened that had not occurred since the 1930s. Financial institutions that were the bedrock of the American banking system began to collapse in rapid succession. With the Republican Bush Administration taking the brunt of the blame. And what precipitated the sudden collapse was unusual.

The Bush Administration had been bailing out multiple financial institutions over the previous year to keep the nation's financial system from cascading into a complete meltdown. Those institutions had invested heavily in the lucrative subprime mortgage market. When those high-risk borrowers were unable to pay their house notes, it all turned sour in a big way. To stave off financial calamity, the Bush government became actively involved in securing the institutions at risk. Especially since many big banks and financial institutions were so interconnected, creating the potential for a devastating financial contagion. And thus far, throughout 2008, the administration had very adroitly and successfully succeeded in preventing the worst from happening through bailouts.[11]

But with only six weeks remaining in a presidential election, the Bush Administration suddenly refused to bailout a key institution. It was the highly interconnected investment banking giant Lehman Brothers. Whose collapse was guaranteed to cause the financial contagion they had so successfully prevented thus far. As a result, the sudden shift in policy caused the worst financial collapse since the 1930s. The decision not to help Lehman Brothers is credited to Treasury Secretary Hank Paulson. As a former CEO of Goldman Sachs, one of the most connected financial institutions in the world. (Think New World Order.) Paulson singlehandedly enabled this collapse with his decision to suddenly reverse policy.[12] A policy reversal the liberal *New York Times* would scathingly take him to account for. Wondering why he suddenly changed course and blaming him for the collapse that followed.

Mr. Paulson's sudden policy shift not only precipitated the worst financial-banking crisis since the 1930s, but also resulted in something else just as predictable. A panicked electorate blamed Bush and his party — the Republicans—for the issues that followed. It was as though Mr. Paulson wanted to kill the chances of the Republican candidate. Or, put another way, to elect the unknown senator from Illinois to the presidency. And that is exactly what happened.

The Hidden Kingdom

It is apparent from the record of how Mr. Obama rose to power that there was a powerful force behind him. One able to void the candidacies of an incumbent state senator along with three others vying for office. Demonstrating a powerful corrupt influence on a local level. Then, on a statewide level, that same force was able to drive two powerful Illinois politicians out of a U.S. Senate race. Leaving that high and coveted political office, Mr. Obama's for the taking.

On a national level, it had the power to block all others and grant the keynote speech at the 2004 Democratic National Convention to then-State Senator Barack Obama. Elevating the unknown Mr. Obama to the national stage and rocketing him past a multitude of long-time Democratic politicians. This hidden force was then able to coordinate major media to elevate his speech before the American people. On que, declaring it one for the ages, and preparing the way for his 2008 presidential run. And, most ominously, on a national and international level, it was powerful enough to prevent a critically important bailout from being implemented. Precipitating a national and international financial collapse that impacted the lives of millions of people across the world. For what appears to be the sole purpose of electing Mr. Obama President of the United States. And, finally, not long after assuming office, he received the Nobel Peace Prize. For the first time in its history awarded to a person before they did something. What influence!

Conclusion

As obvious as it is that some ultra-powerful force moved behind the scenes to catapult Mr. Obama into the White House, that fact alone isn't enough to make the case that he was a Manchurian President serving at the pleasure of the New World Order/Beast Kingdom.

However, when the knowledge of his highly controlled and choreographed rise to power is placed in context with his actions while sitting in the Oval Office, a clear picture develops. A picture of a man placed in high office by a powerful force for the express purpose of bringing America under the control of another kingdom. Conquering America from within and explaining why the nation plunged into spiritual darkness thereafter.

Chapter Fifteen

BARACK OBAMA: SERVANT OF THE BEAST KINGDOM

If the litany of events that unfolded in perfect order to advance Mr. Obama into the White House were not the work of a powerful entity, then, as one commentator was quoted as saying, "Mr. Obama is the luckiest politician ever!" Some may write off his rapid ascension to power as just that. A string of incredible luck. However, when considering the level of "luck" it took to place him in power, alongside the dark deeds he engaged in as president, a more reasonable picture emerges.

Mr. Obama engaged in many actions while president where he appeared to be marching to a strange tune. The Nobel Peace Prize winner directly undermined peace in the Middle East in his first year in office by destabilizing moderate Arab regimes. Resulting in the launch of the "Arab Spring." Ultimately, replacing the moderate Egyptian government of Hosni Mubarak with a Muslim Brotherhood government. The mothership organization and spiritual foundation for Middle Eastern terrorism.[1] But that was just for starters.

In the nation of Libya, Mr. Obama undermined the dictator there too. A dictator who had moderated over the years, becoming a moderating force in the region. Obama successfully got him overthrown under the guise of "democracy." The same kind of radical authoritarian "democracy" Egypt experienced under the Muslim Brotherhood.

As a result, a stable Libya was transformed into a chaotic nightmare. Resulting in death and starvation and a mass exodus of refugees into Europe. A flood that lasted for years.[2] Many commentators with knowledge concerning the impact of overthrowing the Libyan leader, concluded that such an action would destabilize the region. They also predicted a sea of refugees flowing from North Africa. Which was exactly what happened. An invasion comparable to the one at the southern border of the United States. And when considering the main method indicated by the prophet Isaiah in taking down Western nations (covered in the chapter "Trojan Horses") at the beginning of the end times, it all takes on a very sinister shade. Especially since it appears Mr. Obama went against advice in doing so.

He also destabilized the nation of Syria. No friend of the United States but also another nation that was stable. Since Obama's actions, that nation, too, became a living nightmare for its residents. With the horrid radical Muslim group, ISIS, almost taking over the country. An entity some say was created by the United States under Obama. An organization beheading Christians en masse.[3]

All three actions by the Middle Eastern nations had certain common threads. One was the destabilization of non-radical Middle Eastern governments. An action not only against the interests of the United States, but also of its Jewish ally Israel. It also created power vacuums in each nation. Predictably, this provided an opening for radical Muslim regimes to take over. But the "Obama foreign policy" would not end there.

Russia & Ukraine

Russia's invasion of Ukraine in 2022 has caused good people to be up in arms with anger. And rightly so. Such invasions bring death, destruction, and misery to countless innocent people. But with the effective loss of a free press in America, few people understand the important background facts surrounding that war. A story that takes us back to the year 1990 and the fall of the Berlin Wall.

Ending the "Evil Empire"

With the literal crumbling of the Berlin Wall, so, too, did the Soviet Union. The "evil empire" spoken of by President Reagan was eventually broken by the determined president. And as one stabilizing force after another within the empire crumbled, it soon became apparent that such instability was even more dangerous. As such, western leaders began making commitments to the government of Russia to guide it into a soft landing.

Declassified documents show that solemn security assurances against NATO expansion eastward were given to Soviet leaders by major Western leaders. Such as Secretary of State James Baker, President George H.W. Bush, West German Foreign Minister Genscher, Prime Minister Kohl, U.S. Secretary of Defense Gates, French Prime Minister Mitterrand, British Prime Minister Thatcher, and later Prime Minister John Major.

One of the more memorable statements issued by Baker was the commitment of "not one inch eastward" by NATO, given to then-Soviet leader Mikhail Gorbachev on February 9, 1990. With a multitude of those assurances, the troubled Soviet leadership agreed to allow German reunification. And for some time, western leaders abided by their agreement. Until George W. Bush.

It was George W. Bush who began violating the agreement made by his father. But it took Mr. Obama to bring those violations to a new level of severity. Whereas Bush began allowing various East European nations to join NATO — a direct violation of the "not one inch eastward" commitment his father's Secretary of State[4] had made — Mr. Obama went as far as to overthrow the democratically elected government of Ukraine in January 2014. The apparent reason. The Ukrainian government chosen by the people would not allow NATO bases on its border with Russia. Knowing how provocative such an action would be. As a result, the Nobel Peace Prize winner used the CIA to foment a "color revolution" to overthrow the government. An incredibly destabilizing action. And two months after the U.S.-sponsored coup, Russia invaded Crimea in response.[5]

The war that broke out in 2022 with Russia invading Ukraine is a brutal one. A heinous action, regardless of all the provocations by Mr. Bush and Mr. Obama. The loss of life is measured in the hundreds of thousands. With people displaced from their homes registering in the millions. Once the war began raging, a reasonable person would expect Mr. Biden's government to focus on ending it by pushing hard for a peace settlement. But that is not what happened.

Obama's vice president, who "won" the presidency in 2020, literally made it his government's policy to prevent peace between Russia and Ukraine. Actively preventing the Ukrainian leader from engaging in peace negotiations with his Russian counterpart.[6] A dark first for U.S. foreign policy. But Mr. Biden's actions would become much more aggressive than just preventing peace. He would risk war with Russia by engaging in an act of war.

As reported by award-winning journalist Seymore Hersch, elements within the Biden administration plotted and then executed blowing up a pipeline carrying natural gas from Russia to Western Europe. The Nord Stream II gas pipeline. An expensive piece of energy infrastructure resting in international waters that was used to supply natural gas to Germany and France.[7] Since there was no state of war between the United States and Russia at the time of the attack, that action likely qualifies as an act of international terrorism. One that, by any measure, appears designed to start a major war. An action so out of line with American interests as to indicate "someone" or "something" is directing the military of the United States. Consider the sad litany of actions associated with Ukraine by the Obama-Biden administrations.

In January 2014 Mr. Obama destabilized the region by overthrowing the Ukrainian democracy in a violent coup to install an anti-Russian puppet leader. Later, after Russia invaded Ukraine, Mr. Biden prevented real peace negotiations from taking place to end the conflict. Both Mr. Obama's and Mr. Biden's actions reflect a common immoral foreign policy. One that has more in common with Germany's foreign policy during the late 1930s than the typical foreign policy of a republic. Their actions significantly contributing to the loss of life and destruction of property. And later, Mr. Biden's actions in blowing up the Nord Stream II pipeline risked starting another world war.

All of these actions by both men reflect a dark nature that no moral American president would ever consider engaging in. Is it a coincidence that Mr. Obama's rise to power appears to have been orchestrated by a powerful hidden force? And that Mr. Biden would "win" the most tainted presidential election in U.S. history? Those questions raise the specter of who it is that both men serve. And all of this raises a simple question. Why has Russia become such a target for the New World Order/Beast Kingdom?

The answer to that question is that it is almost certain that the New World Order/Beast Kingdom does not control Russia. Two realities tell us this. The first is that Russia would not allow western "vaccines" within its borders. In fact, the Russian vaccine, called Sputnik, was adopted in nearly 70 nations. And reports of major health issues similar to those related to the shots administered in the West have not surfaced. The second reason has to do with the spiritual.

With many nations across the globe being pushed to normalize homosexual and lesbian relationships—in direct conflict with Biblical truth and nature—Russia passed a law in 2013 making it illegal for anyone to promote same-sex relationships. And the law has teeth, with expensive fines against individuals and corporations in violation.

Obviously, no nation under the yoke of the New World Order/Beast Kingdom would contemplate such a law. Nor would a nation under the control of the New World Order/Beast Kingdom have resisted the Western "vaccine."

Oppression at Home

Obama would also engage in actions domestically that no previous president had ever contemplated. And President Trump would find out the hard way. Within the United States, he weaponized both the FBI and the Department of Justice. He did this by placing in key positions individuals whose loyalty is dedicated to going after the enemies of the Democratic Party. A party that has evolved into the political focal point of spiritual darkness in America. A party no <u>true</u> Christian can follow. With those key law enforcement agencies compromised, they were able to undermine the Trump presidency. Actions that resemble organized treason in fulfillment of 2 Timothy 3. Wherein we are told "traitors" will abound within nations in the "latter days." But as bad as Mr. Obama's actions were in terms of undermining peace abroad and democracy at home, it was within the spiritual realm that he best served the New World Order/Beast Kingdom.

Fundamentally Transforming America

There is a reason why Mr. Obama repeatedly stated during his 2008 campaign his intention to "fundamentally transform the United States of America."[8] And his making this statement could not have been a political ploy to gather more votes. Because it raised questions in the minds of voters. Such questions as "transform into what?" The reason for such a brazen statement appears to have been related to the spiritual. A thinly veiled warning of what he intended to do to the people of the

United States. Actions the vast majority of Americans would have rejected if clearly spelled out to them. But only under the satanic doctrine of thelemic occult magic was his statement necessary. An open warning that was issued to negate nature's thrust back against him under that dark belief system.

And there was his announcement during his presidency that America was no longer a Christian nation. An odd statement until placed within the context of spiritual warfare. A statement from the nation's leader that had to echo deeply within the spirit realm. Did his words on a spiritual level turn America over to the New World Order/Beast Kingdom? The same entity that Wilson, Quigley, and many other influential people acknowledged? The one that finally became powerful enough to methodically place Obama in power. Is this why, after he made those spiritual statements, there was a marked increase in satanic ceremonies appearing on nationwide TV at events like the Grammy Awards? Was his lighting up the White House in the rainbow colors of homosexuality an act of turning over the nation to that spirit? Explaining why that sin began spreading like wildfire during and after his second term.

These questions and more beg the same answer. Was Mr. Obama on a spiritual mission as president? Odd for a president unless that was what was demanded by the entity that placed him in power. One dedicated to moving America away from biblical faith. But as significant as all of those grand actions against the God of the Bible were, an even greater reality unfolded behind the scenes.

The Anti-Biblical President

The entire litany of anti-Biblical actions during his presidency is far too numerous to record here. But the following is a good sample of what transpired behind the scenes during his administration. A literal hot war against God. Those actions include his appointing a transgender person to the Advisory Council on Faith-Based Neighborhood Partnerships in an act of disdain for people of faith.[9] When a Young Marines chapter in Louisiana mentions God in their oath, he defunds them.[10] A pastor who was discovered to preach on the Biblical definition of marriage was pressured out of praying at the inauguration.[11] Mr. Obama excluded religious-related service from the student loan forgiveness program. Singling them out.[12] He took a stand against the First Amendment, which protected churches in hiring according to their standards.[13]

When it came to a former president, he forbade Franklin Roosevelt's famous D-Day prayer to be exhibited at the WWII Memorial because it references God.[14] He misquoted "E pluribus unum" ("In God we trust," the national motto) as though he could not allow himself to speak it.[15] And on no less than seven occasions, he omitted the words "the Creator" when quoting the Declaration of Independence. In line with such actions, he refused to host the traditional National Prayer Day at the White House.[16] When speaking at Georgetown University, he ordered a monogram symbolizing Jesus' name to be covered before delivering his speech.[17]

In an act of disrespect, he nominated three pro-abortion ambassadors to the Vatican. All three were rejected.[18] In speaking about Christians, Obama would say they "cling to guns or religion" and don't like "people who aren't like them."[19] When one of those Christians — Delta Force Lt. General Jerry Boykin — was to give a speech at a military prayer breakfast, he was canceled due to his belief in marriage being between one man and one woman.[20] Following orders from his Commander in Chief, an Air Force commander had a 33-year Air Force veteran forcibly and physically removed by four other airmen because he attempted to use the word "God" in a speech.[21] And the litany goes on and on.

At Maxwell Air Base Gideon Bibles were banned. At counter-intelligence briefings, soldiers were told evangelical Christians are a threat. And that donating to such a group could result in military punishment.[22] Heterosexual couples were denied paid leave to marry that homosexual couples were granted.[23] A drag queen was invited to an Air Force base to correct the views of traditional marriage that airmen held.[24] Obama strongly objected to an amendment in the Defense Authorization that protected the religious liberty of soldiers.[25] An Air Force officer was told to remove his personal Bible from sight.[26] At a briefing, U.S. Army soldiers were told to equate evangelical Christians and Catholics with Al-Qeada and the Muslim Brotherhood.[27] Although Christmas nativity scenes were prohibited, a Stonehenge-like worship center for pagan witches was granted $80,000 to move forward.[28]

Conclusion

There are literally hundreds of additional examples that could be provided of Mr. Obama attacking Christianity. The wealth of information gathered on this topic comes from the Wallbuilders organization. All of these actions detail a president dedicated to purging every vestige of God from the United States. A strange goal for an American president. But not for a man placed in power by another kingdom. A kingdom that follows another god. Satan. Effectively governing the United States for that kingdom. A massively powerful kingdom that carefully choreographed his rise to power. It is almost certainly the same hidden kingdom identified long ago by Wilson and later researched by Professor Quigley. Moving America far along the road of godless authoritarianism.

All of this raises other questions. Such as how the culture within American power circles changed to the point that such an internal defeat was possible. And why are there so many people in positions of power willing to go along with the implementation of godless totalitarianism. Part of that answer takes us back to the Nazi Third Reich and its occult foundation, which came to America.

Chapter Sixteen

HITLER'S THIRD REICH: BRINGING THE BEAST TO AMERICA

eep in the heart of Nazi Germany, a fire rages in the dead of night. Encircling it are legions of the elite Nazi SS. Finely dressed in their uniforms, they are engaged in a ceremony. It is a dedication to the renaissance of Aryan civilization symbolized by the solstice. According to Anton Drexler, co-founder of the Nazi Party, the event is a "visible sign of the return to German thought." Others at the gathering speak about the Nordic pagan deity Baldur, a sun god.[1] Those gathered do not understand that Baldur is a demonic principality.

So embedded was the occult in German circles at that time of the Nazi regime that Reichsfuhrer-SS Heinrich Himmler would appoint a special force called the Hexen-Sonderauftrag. The Witch Division. The task of this strange force was to solve the following riddle. How did the dominant Aryan-Germanic religion of nature (witches) be defeated by the decadent Jewish-Christian religion? Nordic "witches" were thought to be "the guarantors of German faith" and "natural healers." The SS Witch Division's conclusion: Christianity destroyed the original natural German faith by associating it with the devil.[2] A truth any Christian could have told them.

In Stephen Spielberg's Indiana Jones films, the plotline has the Nazis searching for the Holy Grail. In reality, he wasn't far off the mark. It was

Himmler who sponsored a book by Otto Rahn titled *Lucifer's Court*. In it, Rahn presents the case that Luciferianism and witchcraft practiced across Germany in the middle ages represented the nature religion of the Germanic people eradicated by the Catholic Church. With the Knights Templar and Tibetan monks preserving those teachings. In the book, he connects the German people to what he describes as the Indo-Aryan bloodline. A bloodline he believed originated from the lost kingdom of Atlantis.[4]

Although the Nordic and Indo-Aryan occult approaches to German religion differed somewhat. Both were used by the Nazi regime in an effort to forge a national religious identity according to the liking of the Nazi government. And such demonic guidance would account for the regime's murderous rampage throughout Europe and elsewhere. Especially against the Jews who were a special target. The demonic legions giving guidance to the Nazis directed them against the Jews due to the role they were yet to play in Bible prophecy. Eliminate the Jews, and you thwart God's plan! In the summer of 1943, as the fortunes of war began to turn against the Germans, the Regional Education Office of the Nazi Party would publish a pamphlet justifying the Nazis' actions against the Jews.

The title of the propaganda piece, *The Jewish Vampire Brings Chaos to the World,* would depict the Jews as a "world parasite" and that the entirety of World War II was actually a conflict between Aryans and Jews, who had "propagated political and economic black magic for three millennia." Claiming that "wherever a wound is ripped open on the body of a nation, the Jewish demon always feeds in the sick place."[5]

Hitler for his part, was demonically guided against the Jews years earlier in *Mein Kampf.* His rambling discourse laying out his plans for Europe and the Jews that apparently only Winston Churchill read. In it, he zeros in on the Jews with invective that years later he would use to justify his mass killings of them. A statement he made in December 1941 concerning the Jews appears to sum up this justification. Saying that "he who destroys life is himself risking death."[6] Since he viewed the Jews as destroying life, he had his justification. But behind all of this was something much greater than simply misguided ideology. It was Satan.

The evidence of Hitler and his henchmen being steeped in the occult goes much further than what has been presented here. But understanding the Third Reich and its evil leader is not possible without understanding their spiritual foundation. It was demonic to its core. A forerunner to the Antichrist and the Beast Kingdom that will be even more demonically twisted. And there is a difference between Hitler's evil kingdom and the New World Order/Beast Kingdom that is worth noting. Whereas in his ambitions Hitler committed genocide against non-German people groups. The unleashing of COVID-19 and the "vaccine" in its aftermath was indiscriminate genocide. Perfectly in line with the expectations that the Beast Kingdom would be the worst in history.

But there is another side to Hitler that must be explored as well, relative to the coming Antichrist. As will be the case for the Antichrist, Hitler, too, had some strange power behind him. A power able to keep him alive until he fulfilled his dark mission. In Revelation 13, we are told the Antichrist will be "wounded to death" and that the world will see that "his deadly wound was healed." In the case of Hitler, he was never resurrected from death. But he was protected from death until he could fulfill his dark mission. We know from Scripture that the Antichrist will come back to life after suffering a deadly wound. But consider the case of Hitler and his many brushes with death as a forerunner to the Antichrist.

Get Up and Move Now!

In the trenches of France during World War I an Austrian corporal is sitting with about thirty of his comrades. They are eating what provisions the German army is able to supply. As he would recall years later,

Hitler heard an audible voice telling him to get up and move away from the gathering. Under such urging, he moves a good distance away from the other soldiers. After settling down to finish his meal, a moment later, a British artillery shell lands in the middle of the soldiers, killing them all. Hitler is saved.[7]

Point Blank!

As World War I is winding down, a British sergeant is amazed as he notices a German soldier coming within easy shooting range of his position. The clearly lost soldier continues to come closer until he is at point-blank range. It is Hitler. The two stare at one another, the sergeant's rifle trained on the German's chest. They clearly see each other's faces in an unforgettable moment. Hitler's life is for the taking. But the soldier does not fire. Instead, he allows the German to live. Years later, he stated that his justification for not shooting was that the war was almost over.[8] Later, as Hitler rose to power, the two men would communicate. Hitler, for his part, would secure a picture from the British soldier. Ironically, Neville Chamberlain, the architect of the catastrophic policy of appeasement that allowed Hitler to rise, would see the British soldier's photograph on one of Hitler's walls.

The Snow Storm

Sometimes small and powerless people have better insight than leaders. As a German carpenter watches the rise of Hitler, he sees great danger. As Hitler stands for election as President of Germany, this carpenter happens to be hired to build a stage from which the Nazi Party leader will speak. He does so and places a bomb directly under the place where Hitler will stand. The bomb is set to detonate 30 minutes after Hitler begins speaking. But for the first time, the long-winded Hitler ends his speech after only 20 minutes. The reason. A great snowstorm is engulf-ing Germany. Unless Hitler leaves the rally early, he will miss his next campaign stop. Ten minutes after Hitler is gone, the bomb explodes. The brave carpenter is ultimately found and killed.[9]

Valkyrie

The motion picture starring Tom Cruise is real. Hitler is saved from a plot against his life by the fact that the bomb planted under a confer-ence table he is gathered around was moved at the last moment behind a thick oak table leg. Multiple people in the room are killed. But Hitler sustains relatively minor injuries.[10] And not long before that attempt, some German generals took the opportunity of Hitler's visit to the east-ern front to kill him. Placing an altitude bomb in the aircraft he flew out on. When the craft reached a certain altitude, it was supposed to detonate, ending the life of the monster. But it does not trigger for some reason. Hitler is saved again.[11]

Are these escapes from certain death all just coincidences? Or part of a larger picture where a wicked man was supernaturally protected by Satan? A foreshadowing of the Antichrist, who will be empowered by Satan. Which means there will be a host of supernatural events taking place around him. Not just to save him from destruction, but to em-power him to destroy on a grand scale. Hitler, as a foreshadowing of the Antichrist, destroyed on a scale never before seen. Of the destruction to be wrought by the Antichrist, we are told this by Daniel.

…and he shall destroy wonderfully…

Hitler had a strong drive to destroy the Jews. Killing them en masse with German efficiency. Being guided by Satan and as a foreshadowing of the Antichrist, it is not surprising he went after them. Because con-cerning the Jews, Daniel tells us what the Antichrist will also do.

...and shall destroy the mighty and the holy people.
Daniel 8

In terms of his political abilities, Hitler's exceeded those of his fellow German politicians. As a corporal in the German army and a painter, he rose to be the leader of the German nation. A feat that almost certainly involved strong supernatural intervention. Then, after using democratic means to achieve his goal of becoming chancellor of the nation, he engaged in crafty acts of deceit to dissolve the democracy that placed him in power. Replacing it with himself as dictator. Not only did he clearly possess an understanding of schemes and deceits on a level beyond that of his contemporaries. But he was also a fierce character to look at. Possessing piercing blue eyes and a stern look of command. Here, too, these characteristics are a forerunner to the Antichrist. Consider Daniel 8, which provides the same description of the Antichrist.

> [23] And in the latter time of their kingdom, when the transgressors are come to the full, a king of fierce countenance, and understanding dark sentences, shall stand up.

Part of Hitler's appeal was his ability to mesmerize crowds of people through his speaking skills. Again, skills on a level that was vastly beyond those of others at that time. So much emotional energy would he exert in the delivery of those speeches that he would be soaked in perspiration afterward. Great speaking abilities are another trait the Antichrist will possess, as detailed in Daniel 11.

> [21] And in his estate shall stand up a vile person, to whom they shall not give the honour of the kingdom: but he shall come in peaceably, and obtain the kingdom by flatteries...

He uses his mouth to speak "flatteries." And also "great words."

> ²⁵ ...And he shall speak great words against the most
> High. Daniel 7

From the perspective of making war, Hitler also fulfilled the role of an Antichrist foreshadowing figure. Bringing about war after war until Europe, Africa, and the seas went up in flames. So it will be with the Antichrist. As noted in Daniel 11 and the Book of Revelation, he will be engaged in countless wars of aggression until he meets his end at Armageddon. Hitler's Armageddon was in Berlin in 1945. The Antichrist's will be on the plains of Megiddo.

We know from many researchers that the Hitler regime was deeply involved in the occult. In addition to Hitler, other top Nazi leaders, such as Heinrich Himmler, head of the feared SS, and his deputy Reinhard Heydrich, openly engaged in dark ceremonies and rituals as part of exercising the black arts. An example was the occult ceremony top SS men engaged in before Operation Barbarossa.[12] The brutal Nazi invasion of Russia. In such ceremonies, the Nazi SS dagger would play a prominent role. Opening the door to deep demonic guidance. It is no coincidence that this guidance led to the murder of millions of people, especially Jews. Aiding Satan's efforts to thwart Biblical prophecy.

To understand the Nazi influence that was brought into America after the war is to understand why certain institutions have become so corrupted. Powerful institutions that are now controlled by minions of the New World Order/Beast Kingdom. It may also explain the moral degeneration of the national news media, which now act in unison to create false narratives detrimental to the nation, just as the Nazi propaganda machine did in Germany. It also explains the authoritarian turn within institutions such as the F.B.I. and the D.O.J. Acting more like branches of a political party than a law enforcement agency in the same way that was done in Nazi Germany. It may also explain why during a "pandemic" medicine reported by front-line clinics as effective in treating the virus was withheld. Costing countless lives. This speaks to the corruption of medical organizations, where political narratives rise above saving lives. Also, why was such a pandemic used in a way that had more in common with a mass psychological operation than a medical response? Why threats were used to replace medical science with political science. Another common thread with the Nazi Third Reich.

The importing of top Nazis into the United States is certainly part of the answer to those and many more questions. Why things have taken such a dark turn over the last several decades as their influence seeped into the halls of power. Did these former Nazis till the soil for the Beast Kingdom to take over the most powerful agencies within the United States government? Compromising the morals and ethics of the nation, making it ripe for the taking?

Hitler & the Nazis: Forerunners to the Antichrist & the Beast Kingdom

The Beast Kingdom is occult to its core. Just as the Nazi regime was. It will kill on a massive scale, even beyond what the Nazis were able to accomplish. It will have a leader even more evil than Hitler, if that were possible. And, apparently, it is. The dark kingdom will challenge God himself. But why is this comparison of the Nazi regime and Hitler to that of the Beast Kingdom and its leader so important?

It is because after World War II, the United States intelligence and scientific communities brought within their inner circles Nazi elites for their knowledge and information.[13,14] Desperately seeking them before the Soviet Union could get their hands on them. But by succeeding in doing so, there is no doubt these former Nazis brought with them their dark occult influences. Possibly, explaining why, since that time, the C.I.A. has become involved in a series of black deeds harmful to America.

Notable researchers have concluded that the C.I.A. was involved in the assassination of President Kennedy. History now records that the C.I.A. was behind the Gulf of Tonkin incident. What we now know was a false flag operation designed as a justification for America getting into a disastrous war in Southeast Asia. Something President Eisenhower had warned against. It may also explain why the C.I.A. falsified reports of "weapons of mass destruction" in Iraq. Resulting in that region being lit on fire as well. And why it overthrew the democratically elected government of Ukraine in January 2014.[15] No doubt on orders from Mr. Obama. Eventually leading to an outright war between Ukraine and Russia. It may also explain why the CIA's domestic offshoot, the National Security Agency, has established a web of surveillance across America, violating the rights of all citizens. All of this leads to an obvious question. Who is really directing the actions of these shadowy organizations? Whose interests are they acting on behalf of? Have they become tentacles of the New World Order/Beast Kingdom? A kingdom in itself that lurks in the shadows.

A Side Note: Digging Up a Nazi Grave

If ever there was ever a regime that symbolized genocide, it was that of the Nazi Third Reich. Not only did they launch wars of aggression that lit the world on fire, but they also methodically exterminated various groups that came within reach of their talons. As a movement that returned German leadership to its occult roots, the Nazis represented the most Satanic regime of modern times. Especially the feared SS, whose occult ceremonies were used to conjure dark forces — much as Satanists continue to do to this day. Critical to the rituals of Satanists are artifacts and objects to which they attribute special powers. Which leads to a strange story that unfolded in early December 2019.

On a cold December night in 2019, grave robbers entered Berlin's Invalids' Cemetery, located in the central part of the city. Their target: the grave of a gloriously buried Nazi that had rested unmolested since 1942.[16] The year he was assassinated. Buried within its dark confines "rested" Reinhard Heydrich. Second in command of the feared Nazi SS under Himmler. As chairman of the infamous Wannsee Conference that took place in January 1942, Heydrich and his henchmen perfected plans to kill millions of Jewish men, women, and terrified children.

Heydrich was a man with a reputation in Hitler's Third Reich. Earning names such as "the butcher," "the hangman," and "Himmler's evil genius." Before his coffin was closed in 1942, his body was clothed in his full SS regalia, including his SS dagger. An instrument critical for the occult rituals of top SS men. Summoning the forces of darkness in support of their evil plans. Those Satanic events took place at the castle Wolfenstein, referred to then and now as the Temple of Doom. [17]

The feared leader of the Nazi SS thought the castle possessed mystic powers. Turning it into a kind of occult Mecca during his reign of terror. As a result, he held occult-satanic ceremonies there with his 12 SS department heads, including Reinhard Heydrich. The grandest such ceremony took place between June 12-15, 1941. One week before the invasion of Russia (Operation Barbarossa) was to begin. Included within that dark satanic ceremony was a statement by Himmler that any Satanist would have approved. Telling his SS generals that one goal for invading Russia was for the SS to eliminate (kill) 30 million Slavs. A ghastly goal.

Since those days of World War Two and the "Temple of Doom," both Satanists and Neo-Nazis have turned that castle into a dark shrine.[18] And that turns our attention back to the clandestine digging up of Heydrich's grave. What is odd is that only a very few people in Germany knew the location of the grave. Hiding it successfully for 77 years. But those who dug it up obviously possessed information on its whereabouts. Indicating that whoever was behind the grave robbery had help from the upper ranks of the German government. And considering the level of satanic evil Heydrich employed — being the architect of genocide — his dagger buried with him would be considered a powerful artifact for conjuring wicked powers. Such as the launch of another diabolical, planned genocide. And this strange grave robbery happened to coincide with the start of what many people now believe was another planned genocide. The release of the COVID-19 virus in early December 2019. So what is the point of telling this story?

There is little doubt that if COVID-19 was a planned pandemic, as many informed observers now believe — genocide — that there must have been satanic influence associated with it from the all-powerful New World Order/Beast Kingdom. A kingdom clearly satanic at the top. There is no other entity on earth as diabolical and evil as it has shown itself to be. Nor is there any entity whose powerful tentacles stretch across the entire world, seemingly into every major power center. If the New World Order/Beast Kingdom was behind the release of the virus, then it is almost certain they would have engaged in a dark ritual or ceremony to launch their genocidal plan. What better artifact to include in the ritual than the same Nazi dagger associated with the man who planned the genocide of the Jews?

Perhaps it is a coincidence that Heydrich's grave was dug up and his coffin opened at the same time COVID-19 was being released. A grave that rested unmolested for 77 years. That is possible. But as the late Biblical scholar Chuck Missler would say, quoting the Jewish sages, "Coincidence is not a kosher word."

Chapter Seventeen

OPERATION PAPERCLIP: A DEAL WITH THE DEVIL

A s the Second World War was winding down, the perspectives of the Allied nations began to be redirected toward the post-war world. With the dramatic increase in Soviet strength, both military and industrial, during the war years and its stated desire at Allied conferences to dominate Eastern Europe, it was becoming apparent to both the United States and Great Britain that their wartime ally would soon become their post-war challenge. So the eyes of Western leaders then turned to their foe, the Germans.

The German scientific community had been highly regarded in various fields of science, especially in the new realm of rocketry. And rockets appeared to be the next logical military step to take at the time. Who better to help develop a nation's rocket program than those most advanced in the art of this burgeoning new science? And there were also the Nazi intelligence services. With all of the efficiency the Germans are known for, they were by far the best intelligence agency in the world when it came to the Soviet Union. As a result, a race began between the major allied nations to capture as many German scientists and intelligence assets as possible. The codename for rounding up German scientists was "Operation Paperclip."[1] However, the operation to capture and use Nazi intelligence leaders was never given a code name. Perhaps because many had hailed from the odious SS.

German Rocketry

In the field of German rocketry, pioneers such as Werner von Braun drove the Nazi program decades ahead of the rest of the world. By the war's end, proof of that reality could still be found on the streets of London, where exploded V-2 rocket parts lay about. With the graves of their victims still fresh on V.E. Day. Those rockets had been built by slave labor at the Nordhausen facility. A factory that produced civilian killing machines, of which von Braun was in charge. Targeting civilians and running a slave labor factory are both war crimes punishable by death. Crimes that violated the basic standards of humanity. Instead of von Braun being prosecuted for his crimes, he was promoted to run the U.S. rocket program.

But von Braun only represented the beginning of criminal Nazis being allowed to escape justice and enter the United States to live the good life. As the scientific community closed its eyes to their new-found colleagues — not hearing, seeing, or speaking any evil about the German scientists — American intelligence was engaging in the same practice. Such was the burgeoning threat of the powerful Soviet Union that lapses in moral judgment became common.

American Intelligence Agencies

Nazis like Dr. Theodore Benzinger were not only given a pass but, in his case, employed by U.S. intelligence. Even though during the war he had worked closely with SS Chief Heinrich Himmler. A real-life monster who's frightful SS had organized the gas chambers that took the lives of countless people. For good reason, Benzinger had been on the original list of war criminals set to stand trial at Nuremberg. But he never saw the inside of a jail cell.[2]

The single most critical person responsible for importing Nazis into the United States was the head of American intelligence, Allen Dulles. Later becoming the Director of the Central Intelligence Agency. There is a certain encounter Dulles had with a Nazi general near the war's end that typifies the attitude of looking the other way when it came to war crimes for the sake of expediency. It is the case of SS General Karl Wolff.[3]

The Nazi General

Nazi general Karl Wolff headed a large contingent of SS troops in Italy at the end of the war. And he was a most odious character. As Himmler's Chief of Staff, he helped set up the train network that carried millions of Jews to concentration camps, where shortly thereafter they were gassed. As a high-ranking member of Himmler's staff, it is not possible that he did not know what was going to happen to them. But that didn't stop Dulles from wanting to bring him on board.[4]

As the war raged, Dulles met with General Wolff in Zurich, Switzerland. It is reported that Dulles, who spoke fluent German, had a very nice fireside chat with Wolff as they sipped expensive Scotch whiskey. Thereafter, Dulles sent cables to Washington lauding Wolff as a "moderate Waffen-SS Nazi" whom the U.S. could work with. A "moderate" whose role in mass killings would have likely caused him to face the death penalty at Nuremberg.[5]

All in all, it is estimated that approximately 1,000 Nazi intelligence officers became part of the C.I.A. after the war. How did so many circumvent justice? By the process of altering the reality of who they were and what they did during the war. All of this to avoid scrutiny and justice. Their records were cleansed, and in some cases, they were given new identities. The C.I.A. became a virtual crime vacuum to hide some very black deeds. One glaring example of this being done is the case of Otto von Bolschwing.

As a top aid to the notorious Adolf Eichmann, he was involved in an array of atrocities. After Eichmann's kidnapping in Argentina in 1960 by the Israeli Mossad, Bolschwing became worried his name would come out during Eichmann's trial. Which it did in the most notorious way. Eichmann credited him with being an early pioneer of methods to terrorize the Jews before the mass killings of them began. Up to his eyeballs in crime, he went back to his C.I.A. handlers for protection. Which they provided.[6] But the C.I.A. was not the only powerful U.S. agency infiltrated by the Nazis. The F.B.I. under Hoover was as well.

Although not inundated with Nazis to the degree of Dulles' C.I.A., Hoover used dozens of them as informants, granting them protection from prosecution in return. Hoover's justification differed from that of Dulles. Hoover, for his part, simply denied in public that these people were Nazis. Claiming that those saying they were Nazis were spreading Soviet propaganda. One such case of Hoover intervening is that of Laszlo Agh. An F.B.I. informant living in New Jersey who, during the war, was a Nazi collaborator in Hungary. According to multiple witnesses and his statements to the F.B.I., he had a propensity to force Jews to throw themselves onto buried bayonets as well as force them to eat their feces. Hoover blocked an F.B.I. agent from testifying to those charges, effectively protecting Agh.[7]

Between Operation Paperclip importation of about 1600 Nazi scientists and the U.S. intelligence agencies' importation of about 1000, the upper power structure of the United States became drenched in Nazi influence. This is especially true of the C.I.A. An agency whose basic power structure, from the start, many believed was incompatible with a republic. It was President Truman who said its creation was his main regret as president. So you may be wondering how all of this relates to the rise of the Antichrist and the Beast Kingdom. Significantly. And here is why.

The Occult/Nazi Influence in America

After the First World War, the influence of "over there" on American culture was significant. After several million U.S. soldiers had inter-mingled with European culture, it was inevitable they would bring some of it back to the states. Doughboys from Kansas farms and Philadelphia streets experienced Paris in all its culture and risqué opportunities. As such, it is no surprise that the Roaring Twenties launched shortly thereafter. A new expression of American culture that in many ways reflected the ways of France and the French people brought back by the Americans who had fought there. But the impact on America after the Great War appeared to be limited to American culture. Not the halls of government power. However, World War Two would be another matter.

Bringing thousands of Nazis into the top tiers of both the scientific and intelligence communities caused something to change in America. On a fundamental level. By the time the early 1960s arrived, prayer had been removed from public schools. Unthinkable to previous generations. Effectively, the government of the United States became anti-Christian. Something the Nazis would have understood. That happened in 1962. Then, in 1963, an American president was killed on the streets of Dallas; the accused killer gunned down two days later while in police custody by Jack Ruby. A man jammed up with Mafia ties. And as an army of citizen researchers and investigators dug deeper into the assassination, it became clear that Oswald had not acted alone. But was part of a much wider conspiracy. But Oswald would not be the only key witness to meet with a sudden death.

As the months passed, a multitude of other witnesses and nosey people would meet a sudden end. All having one thing in common. Their story did not match the official narrative surrounding the assas-sination being produced by the F.B.I. Probably the most notable investi-gator to be done away with was the famous reporter Dorothy Kilgallen.

Kilgallen was the lone reporter to whom Jack Ruby was willing to speak with at length and in private. Thereafter, Kilgallen told friends that she had gotten enough information to show there was a conspiracy behind the president's killing. Her next step was to go to New Orleans to speak to several individuals whose names she would not divulge. Indicating to her hairdresser that it would be dangerous but should break the case wide open. But on the eve of her trip, she overdosed on drugs. Along with her life, all of her papers detailing what she had uncovered also disappeared.

That there was a conspiracy to remove Kennedy that involved elements of both the C.I.A. and the F.B.I. is now taken for granted by almost all researchers of the affair. And this probably accounts for why, even decades later, the C.I.A. still refuses to release all of its files on the assassination. But all of this points to something even more sinister than the killing of a president. It is the transformation of U.S. intelligence and even federal law enforcement into something more recognizable in Nazi Germany than in America before the war. And not long after Kennedy's assassination, what might have been the reason behind his killing unfolded in Southeast Asia.

War after War

On August 2, 1964 — only eight months after the replacement of Kennedy with Vice President Lyndon Johnson — the C.I.A. reported that North Vietnamese gunboats attacked the U.S. Navy ships Maddox and Turner Joy. An act of war! But it never really happened. However, this "false flag" operation embroiled the U.S. in the Vietnam War. After a decade and over a million deaths, it finally came to an end. The C.I.A. would do it again after the attacks of September 11, 2001.

After the September 11, 2001, attacks, which the C.I.A. missed, the agency falsely claimed the nation of Iraq possessed "weapons of mass destruction," which was then used as a justification to invade that country. Although the leader of that country was a bad man, it was apparent he had no role in the attack on the U.S. So the C.I.A. fabricated a threat as justification to invade, resulting in over a million deaths.

This same process would be employed in Ukraine, with the effect of starting another war there. As mentioned earlier in January 2014, under the Obama regime, it was the C.I.A. that was used to overthrow the democratically elected government of Ukraine in what was called a "color revolution." Destabilizing the entire region and eventually embroiling it in conflict.

Nazi Influence

All of these events are pointed out to show how much of an impact Nazi influence appears to have had within the highest circles of American power. How could it be otherwise? Mixing wickedness into a system cannot produce goodness. And it is no wonder that a brief tour of the 1930s shows the exact same pattern of false flag operations, government overthrows, and assassinations by the Nazi regime under Hitler. Actions that were unthinkable in America before the 1960s.

But the impact has not been limited to the intelligence agencies. The press in America after World War II was also impacted. Becoming increasingly controlled by dark forces that collude and manipulate instead of report. That, too, is no different than what the Nazi propaganda machine was about. The Nazi/occult influence appears to have spread into multiple venues of power. Is that influence responsible for the move away from Christian beliefs and toward the New Age movement? A movement as occult driven in many ways as that in Nazi Germany?

The Bigger Picture

But there is an even bigger picture behind all of this. For the Antichrist to take over the world, it was necessary for him to bring America under his wicked wings. As a nation that for decades resisted the darker drives in the world, the importing of Nazi/occult influences into the country in the late 1940s appears to have made America ripe for the taking. Dramatically altering the basic morality and ethics of American leadership.

PART V

ABILITIES AND METHODS
OF THE ANTICHRIST

Chapter Eighteen

WHO IS THE ANTICHRIST?

F rom the title of this chapter, it may seem that the identity of the Antichrist is about to be revealed. Sorry to disappoint. However, in order to make a positive identification, it is necessary to learn about the enemy. The beast has distinctive things he will do that characterize who he is. Making it important to understand some of his actions during his rule as well as the supernatural nature of the times. Obviously, this evil man will have much in common with his father, Satan. Just as Christians should have much in common with their Father, the Lord. One key to understanding the Antichrist is by what he and his father want most. And that is worship. Biblical stories about both of them make this clear. Such a desire is the key to understanding his motives and actions during the end times. To get a handle on this, we begin with the devil paying Jesus a visit in the wilderness.

Worship Me!

Having suffered forty days without food, the hunger pains Jesus felt had to be great. Being fully man as well as fully God, surely He felt their impact. We also know from Matthew 4 that as His forty days were nearing an end, He knew the tempter would come to test His weakened condition. And right on cue, the devil did just that. Immediately upon arriving, Satan spoke tempting words to the Son of God. Temptations that struck directly at Jesus' flesh. Interestingly, he first called into question Jesus' identity. A tactic all true believers are familiar with. "If thou be the Son of God, command that these stones be made bread." Then, continuing along the same line of attack, he tried it again, questioning why Jesus should not thrust Himself down from great heights. Quoting Scripture, Jesus did away with both impertinences. Finally, Satan got to the real point of his visit.

Having been made "the seal of perfection, full of wisdom and perfect in beauty," he was once incredible to behold, according to Ezekiel 28. Until he sought to be equal with God. And on the basis of that laughable proposition, his visit to Jesus takes on proper context.

> [8] Again, the devil taketh him up into an exceeding high mountain, and sheweth him all the kingdoms of the world, and the glory of them;
>
> [9] And saith unto him, All these things will I give thee, if thou wilt fall down and worship me. Matthew 4:8-9

Seeking worship from the holy and just God of all creation, Jesus dismissively sends the rebel off. But the whole affair demonstrates the delusional depth of the wicked one's mind. He actually thinks he should be worshipped. And this twisted desire explains much of what will happen during the tribulation. The main desire of the "man of sin"— the Antichrist whom Satan will empower — is to redirect worship toward himself. An act of eternal damnation for those deceived enough to accommodate. We start with an event wherein the Antichrist seeks to mimic the resurrection of Christ.

The Assassination

In resolving the mystery of "the beast that was, and is not, and yet is" we saw in "The Sixth King" chapter that the Antichrist will suffer an assassination and then come back to life again. It will be an apparent mimicry of Jesus' resurrection. This "miracle" of the Antichrist coming back to life will pull the unwitting to their eternal damnation: "And they worshipped the dragon which gave power unto the beast: and they worshipped the beast, saying, Who is like unto the beast? who is able to make war with him?" This worship is the whole point. Going from death to life again provides the justification for him to be worshiped as a god. But the assassination also does something else.

The assault that takes the life of the Antichrist will devastate one of his arms and disfigure his right eye. Zechariah 11 covers this disfiguration in detail. The prophet refers to the Antichrist as the "idol shepherd." One of the many names used in Scripture for the wicked man.

> Woe to the idol shepherd that leaveth the flock! The sword shall be upon his arm, and upon his right eye: his arm shall be clean dried up, and his right eye shall be utterly darkened. Zechariah 11

Never before has an assassination succeeded only to have the victim return to life. It is a moment so supernatural as to drive the talons of demonic deception deeper into the minds of those who do not know the Lord. After the assassination, his scarred, "dried-up" arm and "darkened" right eye become badges of honor to be emulated by his world of followers. In fact, he orders it. And this plays into the implementation of the Revelation 13 system for complete economic control, as covered earlier. Wherein he requires a "mark" to be placed on the hand or forehead in order for them to engage in the act of buying or selling.

> [16] And he causeth all, both small and great, rich and poor, free and bond, to receive a mark in their right hand, or in their foreheads:

¹⁷ And that no man might buy or sell, save he that had the mark, or the name of the beast, or the number of his name. Revelation 13

The taking of these marks will be an observable sign of allegiance to the Antichrist, acknowledging him as a god and showing sympathy for his wounds. Just as there are many Christians who wear a cross representing Christ's death and resurrection, the locations of these marks do the same in honor of the Antichrist's death and resurrection. These marks also represent his name or his number, whatever that name is. With governments around the world moving toward the implementation of a Central Bank Digital Currency, one that could be turned on and off, along with the mask-wearing mandate during COVID-19, two important pieces of the prophecy puzzle are beginning to fall into place. Ready to be implemented when the time arrives.

All of this shows the character of the beast. He thinks himself a god and will kill anyone who does not agree. His nature is that of a megalomaniac with unlimited pride as a guide. Impulses that gurgled up from hell. And he is faithful to his spiritual father, Satan. These basic features of his character should be present before he rises to the throne of the Beast Kingdom. Features that will be signs of his presence while still mingling among men.

Another Beast Rises

Dark characters always have accomplices. They cannot rise to power without them. Adolf Hitler had many. A prototype of the Antichrist, he surrounded himself with a cast of monsters that will be replicated by the Antichrist. Such accomplices should be one of the main factors used in identifying the Antichrist as he rises. Their complete lack of ethics and morals gives them away. In the case of the Antichrist, he will receive help in obtaining worship from the damned from another beast. During the end times, there will be a multitude of beasts. But one beast will be especially helpful to the Antichrist. He is the world religious leader mentioned in Revelation 13: "And I beheld another beast coming up out of the earth, and he had two horns like a lamb, and he spake as a dragon." And he is no ordinary beast. Like the Antichrist, he has great power. Supernatural power. And he uses it to cause people to worship the Antichrist: "And he exerciseth all the power of the first beast before him, and causeth the earth and them which dwell therein to worship the first beast, whose deadly wound was healed."

There is something eerie about this second beast. Something supernaturally macabre. He has powers typically reserved for science fiction novels. But he is no joke. What he is capable of doing deceives legions of the lost into worshiping the Antichrist.

> [13] And he doeth great wonders, so that he maketh fire come down from heaven on the earth in the sight of men,

> [14] And deceiveth them that dwell on the earth by the means of those miracles which he had power to do in the sight of the beast; saying to them that dwell on the earth, that they should make an image to the beast, which had the wound by a sword, and did live.

> [15] And he had power to give life unto the image of the beast, that the image of the beast should both speak, and cause that as many as would not worship the image of the beast should be killed. Revelation 13

Possibly this second beast does these supernatural wonders through the perversion of science. The use of A.I., perhaps? Or is he empowered by Satan? But regardless of how he does it, the effect appears to be the same. It creates an irresistible draw for the lost to worship the Antichrist. And with all of these supernatural events unfolding across a condemned and lost world, the speaking skills of the Antichrist seal the deal for their souls.

Great Orator

Mankind appears to be easily misled. Adolf Hitler swept the German people off their collective feet in the 1930s. Spellbinding them into committing great acts of terror. The madman murdered on a mass scale. As previously mentioned, like Hitler, the Antichrist will also possess great oratory skills. Revelation 13 tells us: "And there was given unto him a mouth speaking great things and blasphemies." Daniel 7 stresses this as well, telling us he will have" a mouth speaking great things... And he shall speak great words against the most High, and shall wear out the saints of the most High." He is the ultimate blasphemer. Like immoral political leaders who easily deceive legions of the lost through oratory, the Antichrist will do the same but, to a degree, better than most. Setting hooks of destruction ever deeper in the souls of men.

As the Antichrist and the world religious leader are deceiving those who do not know God, they are also persecuting those who do. Revelation 13 tells us how severe this persecution will be: "And it was given unto him to make war with the saints, and to overcome them: and power was given him over all kindreds, and tongues, and nations." But those who know their God will remain faithful, "loving not their lives unto death," according to Revelation 12.

In the Old Testament, the prophet Daniel spoke of this as well. In Daniel 11, speaking of the Antichrist, Daniel tells us that he will... "magnify himself above every god, and shall speak marvelous things against the God of gods, and shall prosper till the indignation be accomplished;

for that that is determined shall be done." The old habit that got Satan thrown out of God's kingdom has completely consumed his Antichrist.

Daniel 11 is a very interesting chapter as it concerns the Antichrist. And it reveals something ominous about him, as was covered in "The Sixth King" chapter. When he comes back to life after the assassination, he is referred to as the "vile person." And in Revelation 17, we ominously find the answer as to why this new description of him is being used. And it is ghastly.

The Entity from the Bottomless Pit

> [8] The beast that thou sawest was, and is not, and <u>shall ascend out of the bottomless pit</u> and go into perdition; and they that dwell on the earth shall wonder, whose names were not written in the book of life from the foundation of the world, when they behold the beast that was, and is not, and yet is. Revelation 17

This verse directly relates to his rising from the dead after suffering the fatal wound described in Revelation 13. After telling us that the beast "was, and is not," we are then told where it is that he ascends from when he rises from the dead. It is the "bottomless pit." What enters the body of the Antichrist when he rises from the dead comes from the horrific "bottomless pit," a holding tank for terrible demonic entities weighted down by chains lurking within its dark abode. Revelation 9 provides some detail concerning these monsters.

> [11] And they had a king over them, which is the angel of the bottomless pit, whose name in the Hebrew tongue is Abaddon, but in the Greek tongue hath his name Apollyon. Revelation 9

These entities in this dark abode have a king. "Apollyon." One such entity possesses the Antichrist after he rises back to life. Making his character one that literally gurgled up from a part of hell. This likely explains why he sits in the rebuilt temple, declaring himself to be God. Then demanding to be worshiped as God. Placing the lives of those who refuse to do so in jeopardy. But he has opposition. And it is supernatural in origin. In Revelation 11, two witnesses are speaking the truth of God to the entire world from Jerusalem during the first half of the seven-year tribulation.

> ³ And I will give power unto my two witnesses, and they shall prophesy a thousand two hundred and threescore days, clothed in sackcloth. Revelation 11

They are witnessing the truth of God to a deceived world. And they bring great plagues across the globe as well. Therefore, they are hated by the world for what they do. And eventually are murdered by the Antichrist.

> ⁷ And when they shall have finished their testimony, the beast that ascendeth out of the bottomless pit shall make war against them, and shall overcome them, and kill them. Revelation 11

Then this stunning supernatural moment happens:

> ¹¹ And after three days and an half the spirit of life from God entered into them, and they stood upon their feet; and great fear fell upon them which saw them. Revelation 11

The Lord resurrects His "two witnesses." It is a Divine slap in the face to the Antichrist and his resurrection. A rebuke by demonstrating two new resurrections. It is especially impressive because "their dead bodies shall lie in the street of the great city," Jerusalem, for three and a half days. And there is little doubt that these resurrections are a real eye-opener for some. Breaking the spell that the resurrection of the Antichrist cast over them.

The Rebuilt Jewish Temple

There is a focal point in the universe that has the eye of the Lord on it. It is the city of Jerusalem. The city where He dwells. Psalm 9:11 speaks to this: "Sing praises to the Lord, who dwells in Zion." And the prophet Joel as well, in Joel 3: "Then you will know that I am the Lord your God, Dwelling in Zion, My holy mountain. So Jerusalem will be holy." But within the city, there is a very specific place that is holy ground. The Temple Mount.

The Temple Mount is where the holy temple of God once stood. Glorious in appearance, it stood as the cornerstone of the Jews' covenant relationship with the Lord until it was destroyed in 72 A.D. We are told in multiple Scriptures that it will stand once again in the end times. Ready to play a sacrilegious role, unwittingly rebuilt to be defiled. Paul, in 2 Thessalonians 2, tells us about this moment. Speaking of the Antichrist: "Who opposeth and exalteth himself above all that is called God, or that is worshipped; so that he as God sitteth in the temple of God, shewing himself that he is God."

In Matthew 24 — Jesus' discourse on the end times — the Savior also tells us what will happen in the rebuilt temple. "When ye therefore shall see the abomination of desolation, spoken of by Daniel the prophet, stand in the holy place, (whoso readeth, let him understand:)" This abominable action desecrates the rebuilt temple. And all this is done for a simple reason. Satan wants to be worshipped. And does so by proxy through the Antichrist.

The horrid moment of the beast sitting in the rebuilt temple — defiling it and using the event to make his false claims — happens at the midpoint of the seven-year tribulation. Thereafter, he unleashes his pent-up fury against the followers of the true God. But in order to defile the rebuilt temple, the Antichrist will first have to possess military control over the holy city of Jerusalem. The prophet Daniel spoke about this control.

> [11] Yea, he magnified himself even to the prince of the host, and by him the daily sacrifice was taken away, and the place of the sanctuary was cast down.

> [12] And an host was given him against the daily sacrifice by reason of transgression, and it cast down the truth to the ground; and it practised, and prospered. Daniel 8

We are told a "host was given him against the daily sacrifice." The Hebrew word for "host" in the verse is the masculine noun "saba," used for an army. Using an army, the Antichrist will capture the city of Jerusalem and the Temple Mount, where the rebuilt Jewish Temple will be located. And then, with military control over the holy city, he will proceed to defile the temple. But what about the rebuilt Jewish Temple, which the Antichrist will defile? Does it have to be rebuilt before the end times can begin? If so, then that would be a roadblock to it beginning soon. The following scriptural perspective says no to that question, removing that roadblock as well. Here is why.

Temple Construction

What we are certain of is that the Jewish temple must be in place and engaging in the ancient Jewish ritual of animal sacrifice no later than the midpoint of the seven-year tribulation. Because that is when the

Antichrist will sit within it. Here is the scriptural perspective that it is re-built during the first half of the seven years, starting with Revelation 11:1.

> ¹And there was given me a <u>reed</u> like unto a rod: and the angel stood, saying, <u>Rise</u>, and measure the temple of God, and the altar, and them that worship therein.

In the verse, the Hebrew word for "reed" is the masculine noun "kalamos." When used in this context, it typically means a "measuring reed or rod," according to Strong's Concordance. A tool of construction. And the Hebrew verb for "rise"—"egeiro"—in this context can also mean "to raise up, or construct," also according to Strong's. Now for the next verse.

> ² But the court which is without the temple leave out, and measure it not; for it is given unto the Gentiles: and the holy city shall they tread under foot forty and two months.

We are then told about a portion of the Temple Mount being given to the Gentiles and that the City of Jerusalem will be tread under foot for "forty and two months." That is the first half of the seven-year tribulation.

Since we are being told about a measuring tool. And to "rise, and measure the temple," which can mean to construct. But to leave out a portion of the Temple Mount from construction. These references appear to relate to its construction. And the reference to forty and two months would have to refer to the first half of the seven-year tribulation since the rebuilt temple must be in place before the midpoint. Just in time for the Antichrist to sit in it and defile it at the midpoint.

The perspective that the rebuilt Jewish temple does not actually get constructed until the first half of the seven years removes a significant stumbling block from the end times beginning. Those who believe the temple must first be in place before the end times can begin, and yet it is nowhere in sight, would mean that its start could not be close. But according to this reading of Revelation 11, construction does not take place until the first half of the seven years.

If this perspective on the rebuilding of the temple is correct, then it removes a major block from the end times being able to begin. The other major stumbling block was removed earlier. That was the need for a ten-kingdom confederacy before the Antichrist could rise. Now we turn our attention to another scriptural perspective relating to certain strange prophetic events that must take place just before the end times begin. Events that are as specific as they are strange and unusual. Various Scriptures will be presented to support that perspective. But as always search the Scriptures for yourself for the truth on these matters to see if you agree.

Chapter Nineteen

MUSHROOM CLOUDS-HEAVENLY WONDERS & "PEACE"

With it likely that the Beast Kingdom has been on earth in its Biblically indicated final form for some number of decades and that the Antichrist is already beginning to make his dark presence felt, our attention turns toward certain signs that are yet to unfold. Specific signs that take place just before the end times thrust down upon the world. Here is a scriptural perspective relating to some very specific events that will unfold just before its launch. As always, search the Scriptures to see if you agree.

A "Peace" Agreement

For one thing, a "Peace" agreement will launch the end times. In 1 Thessalonians 5:1-3 we are told the following about "the day of the Lord."

> ¹But of the times and the seasons, brethren, ye have no need that I write unto you. ² For yourselves know perfectly that the day of the Lord so cometh as a thief in the night.

> ³ For when they shall say, **Peace** and safety; then sudden destruction cometh upon them, as travail upon a woman with child; and they shall not escape. 1 Thessalonians 5:1-3

The verses are clear that there will be proclamations of "Peace" just prior to the launch of "the day of the Lord." And "the day of the Lord," by definition, is the time of the Lord's wrath. We find the confirmation of the "Peace" agreement triggering the seven-year tribulation according to the prophet Daniel. Wherein he, too, tells us the Antichrist will "confirm" an agreement (Peace) launching the seven-year tribulation.

> ²⁷ And he shall confirm the **covenant with many** for one week: and in the midst of the week he shall cause the sacrifice and the oblation to cease, and for the over-spreading of abominations he shall make it desolate, even until the consummation, and that determined shall be poured upon the desolate. Daniel 9:27

The agreement here is described as a "covenant with many." A clue that "many" are involved in it. The confirmation of the agreement by the Antichrist launches the seven-year tribulation. It is also generally accepted that this "Peace" agreement is against the land of Israel. And the Scripture that confirms that is found in Joel 3:2.

> ² I will also gather all nations, and will bring them down into the valley of Jehoshaphat, and will plead with them there for my people and for my heritage Israel, whom they have scattered among the nations, and **parted my land**. Joel 3:2

In this verse, we find "all nations" being punished for a specific action. Because they "parted my land." It appears that "all nations" are the "many" that Daniel tells us are involved in this agreement associated with the Antichrist. For additional context, only three verses earlier, Joel tells us about the launch of "the day of the Lord." This places Joel's parting of the land of Israel in the same time frame as the "Peace" agreement of 1 Thessalonians 5:1-3 and the "covenant with many" agreement of Daniel 9:27. Here is why the parting of the land in Joel must be from an agreement of some kind and not from military conflict.

Notice that nowhere in Joel 3:2 is warfare indicated as the method used to part the land. The word for "parted" in the verse is the Hebrew verb "halaq." A verb that means to "divide, share, plunder, allot, apportion, assign, divide up, distribute, or impart." But nowhere in the lengthy list of descriptions is the word conquered mentioned. The point is that Joel 3:2 is indicating the land of Israel is divided just prior to the launch of "the day of the Lord" without a military fight. Which means it is done by agreement. Further placing Joel's words in context with 1 Thessalonians 5:1-3 and Daniel 9:27. Conclusion: A "Peace" agreement removing land from Israel launches "the day of the Lord," making that event a major end time sign. The other signs involve a strange war with uniquely identifiable characteristics. And this strange war may actually be the justification for the agreement removing the land from Israel in the name of "Peace." That is speculation based on the flow of events about to be presented. As always, you should search the Scriptures to see if you agree. Here is that perspective.

Heavenly Wonders & Mushroom Clouds

According to the prophet Joel, prior to the start of "the day of the Lord," there will be a sign — a strangely unique war. When considering the context of the Scriptures just covered, it would appear that this strange war will take place just before the "Peace" agreement removing land from Israel. Presenting the possibility that this notable and unique war is the catalyst for removing the land. And the war will be notable due to two specific characteristics that the prophet Joel tells us will be associated with it. Both details appear to be qualifiers that allow the generation that sees this war to be able to identify it as the one mentioned in Scripture. Considering all the wars mankind has suffered, those qualifiers were a good idea!

Since this war appears to take place just prior to the "Peace" agreement that launches the end times (the day of the Lord), it is critically important to understand these unusual signs. Especially since one of them appears primed and ready to unfold. The strange war is described in Joel 2:30.

> ³⁰ And I will shew wonders in the heavens and in the earth, blood, and fire, and pillars of smoke. Joel 2:30

About those "wonders in the heavens," there is this. The word used for "wonders" is the Hebrew masculine noun "mopet." A word typically used to signify a miracle of some kind. So when this war happens, there will be some kind of heavenly sign that will be viewed by men on earth as something of a miracle. Exactly what type of miracle we are not told. But for this prophetic war to be positively identified, there must be some kind of miracle event occurring in the heavens associated with it. Now for the other qualifier. Which is an ominous one.

We are told this war will possess "pillars of smoke." Notable enough to be included by the prophet as the second qualifier. But these are no ordinary "pillars of smoke." The Hebrew word used for "pillars" in the verse is the feminine noun "timara." A word that depicts a specifically shaped smoke cloud. One that takes the form of a palm tree. That would be a wide top above a narrow stem. If that sounds familiar, it should. Essentially, Scripture is describing what modern man calls a mushroom cloud. A wide top above a narrow stem. A nuclear mushroom cloud. And this raises the question as to which nations on earth are most likely to launch this war. A unique war, that occurs just prior to the launch of the end times, and that Scripture appears to be telling us will involve the use of some nuclear weapons. Also, a war that will coincide with some form of miracle in the sky as confirmation it is the war noted in Scripture. And the two most likely candidate nations to be involved in this war appear to be either Russia or Israel. First, consider Russia.

Russia

Having violated a multitude of agreements and solemn assurances not to move NATO eastward toward the Russian border, the West has been increasingly antagonizing Russia by effectively attempting to surround the nuclear power with military bases. As a nation that has suffered invasions from Napoleon and Hitler, Russia's sensitivity to these actions creates a dangerous tripwire for a major war. Should war break out between Russia and NATO, and Russia begins losing that conflict, it is quite possible they will use nuclear weapons.

Under such a scenario, should there be the detonation of nuclear weapons by Russia, accompanied at the same time by some strange heavenly phenomena, the words of Joel would come to life. However, such a war involving Russia would not provide the justification for a "Peace" agreement in its aftermath, removing land from Israel. So it is unlikely Russia can completely fulfill this prophecy.

Israel

Israel views the development of nuclear weapons by Iran as an existential threat. And the place where Iran stores this threat — its nuclear facilities and enriched uranium — are caverns located deep under granite-mountains. Rendering conventional weapons ineffective in destroying them. This raises the question of whether Israel would employ the limited use of tactical nuclear weapons in order to deal effectively with the threat. Perhaps by launching nuclear-tipped cruise missiles from their German-made Dolphin submarines lurking under the Persian Gulf. Such a war would fulfill Joel's mushroom clouds. Leaving only the "wonders in the heavens" part of the prophecy to be fulfilled. But it would also do something else.

"Peace"

Under such an attack scenario, Israel would face worldwide hostility on a level never before seen. With the children of Holocaust survivors being accused of doing the same. Nations defending Israel at the U.N. Security Council would run for cover. And this could easily result in a forced "Peace" agreement removing a portion of the Promised Land for the establishment of a Palestinian state. An abomination in the heart of Israel, effectively reversing the Lord's promise of the land to the Jews. The flow of events surrounding an Israeli attack appears to have the best possibility of fulfilling the prophetic scenario presented by Joel. However, as always, it is up to the believer to search the Scriptures to critique or agree with this perspective.

After all of these signs, the world would be on the brink of the end times. And according to Revelation 6, when it launches, the Antichrist will begin riding the "white horse." Wherein we are told:

> ² And I saw, and behold a white horse: and he that sat on him had a bow; and a crown was given unto him: and he went forth conquering, and to conquer. Revelation 6:2

He is "conquering" without a single arrow. As covered previously, he rules the most powerful kingdom in world history. One that has no borders. It derives its power by usurping the sovereignty of nations by infiltrating their power centers with minions loyal to itself. Individuals who either do so knowingly or unknowingly serve it. The "traitors" spoken of in 2 Timothy. And eliminating their national borders as well, in order to allow massive invasions to take place. Clearly, this is something the United States and Western nations, in general, have experienced. Raising many disturbing questions. Such as how many foreign fighters have already entered Western nations, awaiting the order to attack. It is no coincidence that, according to the prophet Isaiah, it is from within that the Antichrist will finish the job of conquering the most powerful nations on earth. And by a tactic once employed by the ancient Greeks. Explaining why the New World Order/Beast Kingdom has ordered its minions to allow the borders of their nations to be left wide open.

Chapter Twenty

TROJAN HORSES

According to various Scriptures, the Antichrist is an "Assyrian" and he is wickedly crafty. Revelation 6 tells of the Antichrist riding the "white horse" as he goes about "conquering and to conquer." But it is in Isaiah 13 that we appear to be told how the wicked man overcomes the nations of the world from this strange and different beast kingdom that he rules.

A Very Dark Sentence

The method used by the Antichrist is a tactic made famous in mythology. It was Odysseus and his Greeks who hid inside a wooden horse brought within the walls of gloating Troy, too busy celebrating the gift to be aware of the treachery that lay within. Falling prey to their own pride. Once inside the impregnable walls protecting the city, the small band of Greeks opened its gates, ensuring its destruction. Like the Greeks of mythology, so, too, will the Antichrist strike nations from within using his own Trojan horses. People from another land who are allowed within the walls of the nations they are destined to destroy.

> 5 They come from a far country, from the end of heaven, even the Lord, and the weapons of his indignation, to destroy the whole land. Isaiah 13:5

The land they come from is a "far country" from the lands they live in and ultimately destroy. Although we are colorfully told they come "from the end of heaven," this is a phrase similar to that also used in Ne. 1:8–9, Dan. 8:8–9, and Jer. 49:36. And each time, it means across the earth and not the Lord's abode in heaven. They are the Lord's "weapons of His indignation" of wrath.

It is those living within the attacked nations who come from a "far country." And Antichrist is the master of "craft" and "dark sentences." He uses deceit and cunning to take down those thought to be impregnable. "They come from a far country... to destroy the whole land." They are his suicidal warriors, awaiting the order to attack. But after unleashing torrents of fire and hell on the nations that took them in, these hunters become the hunted. They suddenly become like "the hunted gazelle" that must "flee to his own land. Everyone" of them!

> [14] It shall be as the hunted gazelle, And as a sheep that no man takes up; Every man will turn to his own people, And everyone will flee to his own land. Isaiah 13:14

They "flee" from the attacked nations for good reason. Because the people of their host countries likely understand who was behind the attack. And target them as a group, causing their mass exodus. Such that "everyone will flee to his own land." And this raises the specter that the attack they launch will be of the highest order in severity, as nothing less would cause such a radical response from the citizens of the attacked nations. The innocent will be targeted along with the guilty. So great will be the rage of those attacked that...

> [15] Everyone who is found will be thrust through, And everyone who is captured will fall by the sword. [16] Their children also will be dashed to pieces before their eyes;

Their houses will be plundered And their wives rav-
ished. Isaiah 13:15-16

A murderous rampage of rage is unleashed against those "from a
far country" suspected of being behind the attacks. So severe is this
response that even "Their children also will be dashed to pieces before their eyes." Their property will be "plundered" along with their
"wives." But there is something odd here. Public rage is not tolerated
by governments to manifest into such widespread mayhem. And that
raises the specter of anarchy. Apparently, the attacks are so severe that
governments are unable to restore order. As such, since there is no
protection, "every man will turn to his own people, And everyone will
flee to his own land." The people "from a far country," which includes
the attackers, "flee" back to their countries of origin. But how can such
Trojan Horses ignite the level of destruction necessary to fulfill these
passages as well as "conquer" a multitude of nations for the rider of the
"white horse"? The answer appears in 2 Peter 3:10.

> [10] But the day of the Lord will come as a thief in the
> night; in the which the heavens shall pass away with
> a great noise, and the elements shall melt with fervent
> heat, the earth also and the works that are therein shall
> be burned up. 2 Peter 3:10

The "sudden destruction of the day of the Lord" described in 1
Thessalonians 5:1-3 comes "as a thief in the night." 2 Peter 3:10 uses
that same "thief in the night" phrase also in describing "the day of
the Lord." And what is described appears to be nuclear devastation.
The detonation of which results in a "great noise," with "fervent heat"
wherein "elements shall melt," such that much "shall be burned up."
These are good descriptions of a nuclear detonation by a first-century
man. Are these descriptions of utter destruction in 2 Peter wrought by

those from foreign lands detonating nuclear weapons? Smuggled within their host nations by warriors of the Antichrist? If so, then it explains at least one reason why the New World Order/Beast Kingdom has ordered their puppet leaders to keep the borders of their nation wide open. They devastate the most powerful nations on earth from within. Against such attacks, there is no defense. As the master of "dark sentences," such an attack is perfectly in line with his wicked nature. Like the COVID-19 attack it all comes from within.

Because we are told it is foreigners living within countries who are used against "all nations," it is clear that the most vulnerable countries to this tactic are the Western "democracies." Nations whose borders have been almost nonexistent for decades. And this conclusion dovetails with Zephaniah's description of those hardest hit.

Western Nations

War is fickle, hitting some harder than others. And according to the prophet Zephaniah (1:14), this great war will be no different. Tellingly, the prophet describes "the noise of the day of the Lord is bitter"—the descriptive used by 2 Peter 3:10 inferring one of the main characteristics of nuclear detonations. He then gives a description of certain nations that are hit especially hard. Their notable characteristics are that they possess the best national defense and intelligence services and are wealthy.

> [16]A day of the trumpet and alarm against the <u>fenced cities</u>, and against the <u>high towers</u>. Zephaniah 1:16

"Fenced cities" signify notable military protection. "High towers" indicate notable intelligence services. And these are wealthy nations. Because "neither their silver nor their gold shall be able to deliver them in the day of the Lord's wrath; but the whole land shall be devoured." (1:18) These nations are consumed "by fire," and it comes from those of a "far country" attacking from within. And those descriptions best fit America and Western Europe. It is this Western block of nations that possesses the strongest military and intelligence services as well as the greatest wealth.

Traitors and Dark Sentences

Open borders bring a flood of death and destruction by increasing both crime and drug imports within the nation. And no loyal American would be opposed to stopping it. This is especially true in light of the attacks of September 11, 2001. Carried out by those from a faraway land with devastating effects. It is the New World Order/Beast Kingdom that has coordinated this policy of national suicide across the West. Demonstrating just how strong its grip over the United States and various Western European countries has become. Such open borders in the age of suitcase nukes appear to be the method that the Beast Kingdom — the New World Order — has decided to use to complete the conquering of nations.

The New Ruler

If the perspective of Isaiah 13 presented here is correct — wherein nuclear weapons smuggled within Western nations seal their doom — then after such detonations, the threat of more going off will hang like a sword over those nations. Not knowing which of their major cities could experience nuclear destruction next. And against what nation can the attacked nations respond? The New World Order/Beast Kingdom has no borders! The conquered must then bend the knee to the new ruler. The Antichrist. Having conquered by employing "craft" and "dark sentences."

As the one holding the "bow" that sends the attacks, the world is unable to trace the arrows back to him. As a result he is not blamed for the devastation but has the ability to stop it and bring "Peace." Causing the world to be amazed by their new savior.

Epilogue

WHEN TROJAN HORSES ATTACK

hen the four horsemen of the apocalypse in Revelation 6 begin their devastating ride, it is the beginning of the end times. The first horse is the Antichrist going about "conquering and to conquer" followed by the other three horsemen. Understandably, that beginning includes descriptions of nuclear weapons, according to 2 Peter 3. All these terrible events come with "sudden destruction," according to 1 Thessalonians 5:1-3.

As the borders of the West remain wide open without regard for who is entering, the number of those coming in to do harm grows by the day. Individuals willing to fly planes into skyscrapers or empty magazines full of bullets into unsuspecting crowds whose only crime is not following their religion. And if those who flew the planes came in legally, how much more danger lurks from those who were never identified? Legions sent through porous western borders from enemy nations with an assigned military task. Yet those whose hands are on the levers of power do nothing.

When that "sudden destruction" finally comes, it is difficult to imagine the United States or Western Europe being spared its horrors. Especially in light of their policies of open borders — a form of national suicide — being in place for decades. As well as having become the focal points of spiritual darkness in the world today. Richly earning the Lord's wrath for having tasted His goodness and then turning to darkness. In fact, in describing the nations hardest hit when the end times start, the prophet Zephaniah appears to be describing the nations of the West. And that means nuclear destruction. Of course, all of this is no real surprise to most students of Bible prophecy. The beginning of the end times will be worse than anything man has ever seen.

Concerning that beginning, there is something I want to share that I believe the Lord has shown me concerning a particular detail relating to it. This was given to me in a dream in January of 2009, and it is very specific. It was by far the most notable of several prophetic dreams I received over a period of years. With each of the prior ones coming to pass as given. However, each of those dreams related to something pertaining to myself or a family member on a personal level. And not toward any grand event like the one I am about to relay.

The Beginning of the End Times

I clearly appreciate and understand the impact of prophetic dreams on those being told. It is far less than for the one who receives them. And this is understandable. Especially since there are so many false prophecies today from those claiming to have received dreams and visions from the Lord. We live in a time when great discernment is required. This unfortunate condition is in line with Jesus' warning at the beginning of His Olivet Discourse (MT 24:4-5). Therein, He tells us the days leading up to the launch of *the day of the Lord* will be ones of great deceit. And who is primarily responsible for this deceit? It is those who come in His name and acknowledge that He is Christ. It comes from elements within the church. But in spite of all the deceit, the gift of prophecy will be granted prior to the beginning of the day of the Lord. The prophet Joel says:

> And it shall come to pass afterward
> That I will pour out My Spirit on all flesh;

Your sons and your daughters shall prophesy,
Your old men shall dream dreams,
Your young men shall see visions.
Joel 2:28

The gift of prophecy is given in the form of "dreams" and "visions." It is His grace and mercy as the most difficult time in human history approaches. Through the Spirit of the Lord "old men shall dream dreams." As for young men they, too, will have their part as watchmen. They "shall see visions." And as the end times draw closer with each passing day, Christians are reporting prophetic dreams and visions they believe are directly from the Lord. But discernment must be employed. Scripture cannot be added to. But details of approaching scriptural prophetic events are given through dreams and visions, according to Joel.

This author is the recipient of one such dream, and it directly relates to a detail on the launch of "the day of the Lord." That is why I am sharing it. Since becoming a believer, I have received several prophetic dreams that I know were from the Lord. Confirmation came not only in their fulfillment but also in the unique nature of each dream. They are remembered in detail for many years, unlike natural dreams. Here is a brief rundown of those dreams. The first came in the middle of the night on the evening I came to Christ. He drew me to Him with a dream of a fierce dragon pursuing me for my life. After waking in a shaken state, I accepted Him as my Savior. And His peace flowed down upon me. The evening prior to receiving the dream, I had tried reading the Bible for the first time in many years. But none of the verses made sense to me. But the next morning, after accepting Christ, the Bible became alive in a way I had never before experienced from any other book. What had previously been confusing was now completely understood. At the time, I didn't realize it, but that was the Holy Spirit now dwelling within me.

The details of that dream that brought me to salvation are still etched in my memory, even though it happened in the mid-1990s. Thereafter,

I received three warning dreams. Two relate to myself and one to one of my sons. Of those prophetic dreams, all three came to pass. Since none of those three warning dreams related to any significant event, but were only personal in nature, there is no point in relaying them. It is the fourth prophetic dream, which is the subject of this epilogue that will impact every person in America and is yet to be fulfilled.

That fourth dream was extremely specific. It was not filled with hazy symbolism wherein one must guess the meaning. But spelled out with complete clarity, allowing only one understanding. And that is part of its disturbing nature. But only part. The other part was the way in which the Lord answered a prayer concerning a particular detail that was not revealed in the dream. A detail of the utmost importance. Here is what the Lord showed me in that fourth dream.

I was clearly shown the detonation of two nuclear weapons within the United States. I was shown the state where it would happen. I was shown the general areas within that state where each would detonate. I was even shown the order of the detonations. The dream also informed me as to the method used to accomplish the attack. How were such specific details relayed? I simply watched as the dream delivered its frightening message. Having received prior prophetic dreams from the Lord, all of which came to pass, this one shook me to my core.

Every significant detail pertaining to the approaching event was given to me except for one. When will it take place? So upon that question, I began praying. For a period of about two months, I prayed the same prayer each evening just before going to bed: "Lord, I pray You will tell me when this terrible day will happen." The prayer was for both curiosity and necessity. Not knowing the timing of this event, I began thinking about what steps to take on a personal level. Should I stock up on food and other essentials? Should I begin alerting others beyond what I had already done? These were only some of the considerations that presented themselves. Then, after praying for about

60 days, a word of knowledge from the Lord came to me in the most amazing way.

Destruction on the East Coast of Florida

The dream came in the morning hours of January 23, 2009. From a bird's-eye view, I was allowed to see two small airplanes flying across central Florida toward its eastern coast. As I continued to watch, I noticed that one of the planes veered on a southerly course inland along the coast. I was then allowed to see the other plane go east toward the area of Cape Canaveral. It, too, stayed inland and not over the Atlantic. My attention was then directed back toward the plane that had turned south. Exactly how far south it had gone I could not see. As my gaze was fixed on it, I saw the sudden detonation of a nuclear weapon. The sight of the detonation included the typical ruthless swirling waves of fire forming a massive fireball — the distinct signature of a nuclear weapon. Then my attention was immediately focused on the other plane flying toward Cape Canaveral.

I could see that the northern plane was located just south of the Cape when another nuclear detonation took place. Once again, the classic fireball associated with the dreaded bomb was as vivid as the first. In line with all other dreams from the Lord, this one became etched into my memory.

Knowing the dream was from the Lord presented me with the prospect of what to do with this knowledge. As a result, I began the process of discussing it with certain friends and family members. But, understandably, the impact on myself was much greater than on those who heard about it from me. This was especially true since I had not shared my previous dreams and their fulfillment with others. However, from the dream alone, I did not know when this approaching day of infamy would take place. That answer would come through prayer and the most unusual spiritual moment of my life.

The Spirit of the Lord

It was a Friday evening, and as I was about to retire for the day, I once again prayed the same prayer: "Lord, I pray you will reveal to me when this terrible day will happen." I then went to bed and slept well.

The next morning, when I awoke, my mind was focused on the various activities of the day. It was a Saturday morning. As I lay awake in bed, considering my day, something in the bedroom began to change.

I became aware of a strong spiritual presence in the room that can only be described as intense goodness. And the intensity of this goodness increased for about a half-minute until it reached a crescendo. Then I heard the quiet, still voice of the Lord speak to my heart the following words: "When they say Peace." It was delivered with complete clarity. Thereafter, I could sense that the goodness permeating the room began to dissipate until, a very short time later, it was completely gone. I continued in bed for a moment, pondering what had just happened.

And as I lay there wondering what had just happened, I began to realize that the Lord had just answered my plea for knowledge on when the nuclear attacks against the United States would happen. It also began to dawn on me that the word of knowledge was straight from Scripture.

When they say, Peace

It is not new that "when they say Peace" "the day of the Lord" will launch. This is given to us in 1 Thessalonians 5:1-3. Wherein Paul informs us that the launch of "the day of the Lord" comes only after "they say Peace." And this is a definitive statement of prophetic truth. He also informs us that the beginning will arrive with "sudden destruction." And 2 Peter 3 gives us a glimpse of this destruction. That it comes not only "as a thief in the night," but will include "a great noise, and the elements shall melt with fervent heat." What was given in the dream is in line with both Scriptures and adds nothing to them. It only describes one of what is almost certainly many locations in the world where devastating destruction will happen.

The description is unmistakably that of nuclear detonations at the 'beginning' of 'the day of the Lord.' And who is setting off these weapons? As we looked at earlier, according to the prophet Isaiah, it is from people who represent a kind of Trojan horse within the nations that are attacked.

> ⁵ They come from a far country, from the end of heaven,
> even the Lord, and the weapons of his indignation, to
> destroy the whole land. Isaiah 13:5

The Antichrist attacks powerful nations from within to bring them to their knees as he goes about "conquering and to conquer." All of the attacks are directed against nations with 'fenced cities, and against the high towers' — a description of the strongest military powers in the world. Here, too, the United States qualifies. We are also told this.

> ¹⁸ Neither their silver nor their gold shall be able to de-
> liver them in the day of the Lord's wrath; but the whole
> land shall be devoured by the fire of his jealousy: for he
> shall make even a speedy riddance of all them that dwell
> in the land.

The nations 'devoured by fire' are also very wealthy. Although they have silver and gold, it is not enough to deliver them. Here, too, the United States qualifies. Although the United States is very powerful, it has also allowed within its walls those who mean it harm.

It is wise to follow Scripture and not the dreams of men. However, it should be noted that the dream is well in line with what Scripture broadly tells us will one day happen. It is nothing more than a dream that supplies a particular detail within that broader framework of prophetic truth. A horrific event that can only take place after specific signs occur. Such as the notable war of Joel 2:30, including heavenly wonders and mushroom clouds. As well as the next event of a "Peace" agreement removing land from Israel. In other words, it will happen only after these other prophetic events take place.

The Approach of the End Times

Many Biblical prophecy students have watched as a multitude of end time signs have begun converging across the globe. And if the Beast Kingdom already exists in the form of the New World Order, as presented here, then the times are even closer than most have assumed. With the Antichrist almost certainly on the scene, which would also provide the best explanation as to why such great darkness has descended upon the world so quickly. Especially, as the COVID-19 virus appears to have been a dry run for assuming great control over the personal freedom of individuals across the world. A top priority of the Beast Kingdom.

What the late President Wilson wrote about in 1913 is known today as the New World Order. An entity that many other high-ranking individuals in America and overseas also spoke and wrote about. But, no doubt, none were aware of how many dark boxes it would eventually check. Boxes that prophecy Scripture tells us the Beast Kingdom would also check. Leading to the point made several times. If the New World Order is not the Biblical Beast Kingdom, then Satan has a house divided. And if the dark curtain descending across the earth is not a sign of the Beast Kingdom as well as the presence of the Antichrist, then what is it?

Salvation

When the end times launch no person alive has a guarantee of survival. It will be a time unlike anything mankind has ever experienced. However, although the flesh of men are at the mercy of a merciless foe, the eternal soul is not. If you have not accepted Jesus Christ as your Savior the time to do so is now!

> [16] For God so loved the world, that he gave his only begotten Son, that whosoever believeth in him should not perish, but have everlasting life.

> [17] For God sent not his Son into the world to condemn the world; but that the world through him might be saved.

> [18] He that believeth on him is not condemned: but he that believeth not is condemned already, because he hath not believed in the name of the only begotten Son of God.

> [19] And this is the condemnation, that light is come into the world, and men loved darkness rather than light, because their deeds were evil. John 3:16-19

References

Chapter One: The Time Has Arrived

1. AZQuotes.com "One World Government" quotes
2. KJV Bible Book of Daniel Ch. 7
3. Newsweek, "Banks Have Begun Freezing Accounts Linked to Trucker Protest," Katherine Fung, 2/18/22, https://www.newsweek.com/banks-have-begun-freezing-accounts-linked-trucker-protest-1680649
4. New York Post, "Australia's insane COVID rules are a warning to the rest of the Free World," Rich Lowery, 9/7/21, https://nypost.com/2021/09/07/australias-covid-rules-are-a-warning-to-rest-of-the-world/
5. US News & World Report, "Obama is wrong when he says we're not a Judo-Christian nation," J. Randy Forbes, 5/7/09, https://www.usnews.com/opinion/articles/2009/05/07/obama-is-wrong-when-he-says-were-not-a-judeo-christian-nation

Chapter Two: The New World Order

1. *The New Freedom*, Woodrow Wilson, 1913, pp 13, Woodrow Wilson, The New Freedom, pp 13,https://books.google.com/books?id=MW8SAAAAIAAJ&pg=PA13&dq=%22Since+I+entered%22+Source:+https://quotepark.com/quotes/1939295-woodrow-wilson-since-i-entered-politics-i-have-chiefly-had-mens/&hl=en#v=onepage&q&f=false
2. AZQuotes.com "One World Government" quotes
3. AZQuotes.com "One World Government" quotes
4. AZQuotes.com "One World Government" quotes
5. AZQuotes.com "One World Government" quotes
6. AZQuotes.com "One World Government" quotes
7. *Philip Dru: Administrator A Story of Tomorrow 1920-1935*, Edward House, 1912
8. AZQuotes.com "One World Government" quotes
9. Carroll Quigley, Tragedy and Hope: A History of the World in Our Time (New York: Macmillan Company, 1966), p. 950

10. *Tragedy and Hope*, Carol Quigley 1965, https://www.zerohedge.com/news/2023-02-19/war-upon-us-all-its-war-we-will-win

11. *A Chronology History: The New World Order* by D.L. Cuddy, Ph.D

12. AZQuotes.com "One World Government" quotes

13. AZQuotes.com "One World Government" quotes

14. AZQuotes.com "One World Government" quotes

15. *The Externalization of the Hierarchy*, Alice Bailey

16. *The Externalization of the Hierarchy*, Alice Bailey

17. *The Externalization of the Hierarchy*, Alice Bailey

18. *The Externalization of the Hierarchy*, Alice Bailey

19. *Humanist Manifesto I*, Charles Potter, 1933

Chapter Three: The Beast Kingdom: Hidden in Plain Sight

1. "The unprecedented consolidation of the modern media industry has severe consequences," The Miscellany News, Helen Johnson, April 29, 2021, https://miscellanynews.org/2021/04/29/opinions/the-unprecedented-consolidation-of-the-modern-media-industry-has-severe-consequences/

2. https://www.researchgate.net/figure/Political-identification-of-college-professors-by-field_tbl1_40823273

3. *The FBI tragedy: Elites above the Law*, National Review, Victor Hanson, June 11, 2019, https://www.nationalreview.com/2019/06/fbi-tragedy-elites-above-law/

4. *Politics and media have critically corrupted the FBI*, New York Post, Victor Hanson, November 18, 2021, https://nypost.com/2021/11/18/politics-and-media-have-critically-corrupted-the-fbi/

5. "FBI Denies any Wrongdoing in Raid, Arrest of Pro-Life Father," Texas Right To Life.com, Peter Pinedo, September 27, 2022, https://texasrighttolife.com/fbi-denies-any-wrongdoing-in-raid-arrest-of-pro-life-father/

6. "Biden's DOJ Threatening Pro-Life Protestors With 11 Years in Jail for Civil Disobediance," The Washington Standard, October 6, 2022, https://thewashingtonstandard.com/bidens-doj-threatening-pro-life-protesters-with-11-years-in-jail-for-civil-disobedience/

7. "FBI Hero Paying the price for exposing unjust 'persecutions' of conservative Americans," New York Post, Miranda Devine, https://nypost.com/2022/09/21/fbi-hero-paying-the-price-for-exposing-unjust-persecution-of-conservative-americans/

8. "Omnibus Shows Congress's Priorities" Authoritarianism & War," Ron Paul Institute, Ron Paul, December 26, 2022

Chapter Four: The Ten Kings: A Ruling Council Initially

Chapter Five: The Sixth King

Chapter Six: A Man of Dark Sentences

Chapter Seven: A Brilliant Dark Plan: The Sign Antichrist is Now Engaging the World

1. Less Than 1 in 100 Million Chance That COVID-19-19 Has Natural Origin: Study By Hans Mahncke Oct 25, 2022 https://www.zerohedge.com/Covid-19-19/less-1-100-million-chance-Covid-19-19-has-natural-origin-new-study
2. David Martin EU Parliament International Covid Summit May 3, 2023, Coronavirus and vaccine crimes, Rumble.com, https://rumble.com/v2mbo8c-david-martin-eu-parliament-international-covid-summit-may-3-2023-coronaviru.html
3. Dr. David Martin w/Brian Rose – Covid Was An Act Of War Against The Human Race (Full Interview), May 2023, Rumble.com, https://rumble.com/v2s2sf6-plandemic-2-indoctornation-by-mikki-willis-with-dr.-david-martin.html
4. David Martin EU Parliament International Covid Summit May 3, 2023, Coronavirus and vaccine crimes, Rumble.com, https://rumble.com/v2mbo8c-david-martin-eu-parliament-international-covid-summit-may-3-2023-coronaviru.html
5. David Martin EU Parliament International Covid Summit May 3, 2023, Coronavirus and vaccine crimes, Rumble.com, https://rumble.com/v2mbo8c-david-martin-eu-parliament-international-covid-summit-may-3-2023-coronaviru.html
6. David Martin EU Parliament International Covid Summit May 3, 2023, Coronavirus and vaccine crimes, Rumble.com, https://rumble.com/v2mbo8c-david-martin-eu-parliament-international-covid-summit-may-3-2023-coronaviru.html

7. Dr. David Martin w/Brian Rose – Covid Was An Act Of War Against The Human Race (Full Interview), May 2023, Rumble.com, https://rumble.com/v2s2sf6-plandemic-2-indoctornation-by-mikki-willis-with-dr.-david-martin.html

8. David Martin EU Parliament International Covid Summit May 3, 2023, Coronavirus and vaccine crimes, Rumble.com, https://rumble.com/v2mbo8c-david-martin-eu-parliament-international-covid-summit-may-3-2023-coronaviru.html

9. Dr. David Martin w/Brian Rose – Covid Was An Act Of War Against The Human Race (Full Interview), May 2023, Rumble.com, https://rumble.com/v2s2sf6-plandemic-2-indoctornation-by-mikki-willis-with-dr.-david-martin.html

10. David Martin EU Parliament International Covid Summit May 3, 2023, Coronavirus and vaccine crimes, Rumble.com, https://rumble.com/v2mbo8c-david-martin-eu-parliament-international-covid-summit-may-3-2023-coronaviru.html

11. Dr. David Martin w/Brian Rose – Covid Was An Act Of War Against The Human Race (Full Interview), May 2023, Rumble.com, https://rumble.com/v2s2sf6-plandemic-2-indoctornation-by-mikki-willis-with-dr.-david-martin.html

12. David Martin EU Parliament International Covid Summit May 3, 2023, Coronavirus and vaccine crimes, Rumble.com, https://rumble.com/v2mbo8c-david-martin-eu-parliament-international-covid-summit-may-3-2023-coronaviru.html

13. Dr. David Martin w/Brian Rose – Covid Was An Act Of War Against The Human Race (Full Interview), May 2023, Rumble.com, https://rumble.com/v2s2sf6-plandemic-2-indoctornation-by-mikki-willis-with-dr.-david-martin.html

14. Plandemic 2, Documentary by Dr. David Martin, May 2023, Rumble.com, https://rumble.com/v2s2sf6-plandemic-2-indoctornation-by-mikki-willis-with-dr.-david-martin.html

15. Plandemic 2, Documentary by Dr. David Martin, May 2023, Rumble.com, https://rumble.com/v2s2sf6-plandemic-2-indoctornation-by-mikki-willis-with-dr.-david-martin.html

16. David Martin EU Parliament International Covid Summit May 3, 2023, Coronavirus and vaccine crimes, Rumble.com, https://rumble.com/v2mbo8

c-david-martin-eu-parliament-international-covid-summit-may-3-2023-coronaviru.html

17. Dr. David Martin w/Brian Rose – Covid Was An Act Of War Against The Human Race (Full Interview), May 2023, Rumble.com, https://rumble.com/v2s2sf6-plandemic-2-indoctornation-by-mikki-willis-with-dr.-david-martin.html

18. Dr. David Martin w/Brian Rose – Covid Was An Act Of War Against The Human Race (Full Interview), May 2023, Rumble.com, https://rumble.com/v2s2sf6-plandemic-2-indoctornation-by-mikki-willis-with-dr.-david-martin.html

19. David Martin EU Parliament International Covid Summit May 3, 2023, Coronavirus and vaccine crimes, Rumble.com, https://rumble.com/v2mbo8 c-david-martin-eu-parliament-international-covid-summit-may-3-2023-coronaviru.html

20. David Martin EU Parliament International Covid Summit May 3, 2023, Coronavirus and vaccine crimes, Rumble.com, https://rumble.com/v2mbo8 c-david-martin-eu-parliament-international-covid-summit-may-3-2023-coronaviru.html

21. Dr. David Martin w/Brian Rose – Covid Was An Act Of War Against The Human Race (Full Interview), May 2023, Rumble.com, https://rumble.com/v2s2sf6-plandemic-2-indoctornation-by-mikki-willis-with-dr.-david-martin.html

22. COVID-19 UPDATE: What is the truth? Russell Blaylock, Surgical Neurological Institute, https://www.ncbi.nlm.nih.gov/pmc/articles/PMC9062939/

23. COVID-19 UPDATE: What is the truth? Russell Blaylock, Surgical Neurological Institute, https://www.ncbi.nlm.nih.gov/pmc/articles/PMC9062939/

24. COVID-19 UPDATE: What is the truth? Russell Blaylock, Surgical Neurological Institute, https://www.ncbi.nlm.nih.gov/pmc/articles/PMC9062939/

25. What is Crimson Contagion?, Brownstone.org, December 22, 2022, www.brownstone.org/articles/what-is-crimson-contagon/

26. What is Crimson Contagion?, Brownstone.org, December 22, 2022, www.brownstone.org/articles/what-is-crimson-contagon/

27. The Wet Market sources of Covid-19-19: Bats and pangolins have an alibi, By Professor David Macdonald, June 7, 2021, https://www.ox.ac.uk/news/science-blog/wet-market-sources-Covid-19-19-bats-and-pangolins-have-alibi

28. Dr. Pierre Kory: The War on Hydroxychlorquine, Ivermectin, and Other Cheap Drugs to Treat COVID-19-19, Jan Jekielek, January 29, 2022, Epoch Times, https://www.theepochtimes.com/dr-pierre-kory-the-war-on-hydroxychloroquine-ivermectin-and-other-cheap-drugs-to-treat-Covid-19-19_4245042.html?utm_source=ai&utm_medium=search

29. Ivermectinissafeandeffective:TheEvidence,ColleenHuber,Dec25,2022TheEpoch Times, https://www.theepochtimes.com/health/ivermectin-is-safe-and-effective-the-evidence_4944960.html?utm_source=ai&utm_medium=search

30. AZQuotes.com Henry Kissinger quote.

31. AZQuotes.com Brock Chisholm quote

32. "How Bill Gates Bought Control Over the WHO," Brightwork Research & Analysis, Shaun Snapp, November 2, 2021

33. Emergency Use Authorization, U.S. Food & Drug, https://www.fda.gov/emergency-preparedness-and-response/mcm-legal-regulatory-and-policy-framework/emergency-use-authorization

34. Vaccine Development, Testing, and Regulation, History of Vaccines, https://his

35. Storyofvaccines.org/vaccines-101/how-are-vaccines-made/vaccine-development-testing-and-regulation

36. The Great Reset: The Perfect Storm, Zero Hedge, By David Solway (PJ Media, https://www.zerohedge.com/geopolitical/great-reset-perfect-storm

37. "Died Suddenly" Documentary https://diedsuddenly.info/

38. "Died Suddenly" Documentary https://diedsuddenly.info/

39. Epoch Times, "Mystery Clots Appear in 50-70 Percent of the Deceased: Funeral Director" Dan Skorbach, September 6, 2022

40. Epoch Times, "Exclusive: Leaked Hospital Memo Reveals 500 Percent Rise in Stillbirths; Fetal Specialist Explains Likely Cause," Roman Balmakov November 2, 2022

41. Epoch Times, "Dr. James Thorp: What Pfizer's Internal Data Reveals About Vaccines and Pregnancy," Jan Jekielek, November, 29, 2022

42. Epoch Times, "Dr. James Thorp: What Pfizer's Internal Data Reveals About Vaccines and Pregnancy," Jan Jekielek, November, 29, 2022

43. Society of Actuaries Research Institute, "2020-2021 Excess Deaths in the U.S. General Population by age and sex." August 2022, https://www.soa.org/4a55a7/globalassets/assets/files/resources/research-report/2022/excess-death-us.pdf

44. "The Great Reset: The Perfect Storm," PJ Media, David Solway, November 7, 2022

45. "Pandemic Dry Run October 2019," Glen Beck

46. "Bill Gates Global Takeover is Official," Mercola, Dr. Joseph Mercola, December 26, 2022

47. https://www.theepochtimes.com/government-creating-a-luciferase-mark-to-track-vaccinations-cdc-admits-myocarditis-risk_4728265.html?utm_medium=email&utm_source=Morningbrief&utm_campaign=mb-2022-10-25

48. "Federal Data Quietly Reveals 100 Terror Suspects Caught at Southern Border," ZeroHedge.com, Steve Watson, October 26, 2022

49. Trump to Keep His Own Private Security, The Daily Beast, April 13, 2017, https://www.thedailybeast.com/cheats/2016/12/19/trump-security-force-playing-with-fire

50. Danchenko trial helps Durham expose how corrupt FBI framed Trump, Fox News, October 17, 2022, https://www.foxnews.com/opinion/danchenko-trial-helps-durham-expose-corrupt-fbi-framed-trump

51. "ICBA Denounces Remarks from Treasury Secretary Janet Yellen on Bailouts for Systemically Risky Institutions," ICBA, Aleis Stokes & Nicole Swann, March 16, 2023

52. "Strange New Respect for Nazi-Adjacent Pagans," ZeroHedge.com, January 01, 2023

Chapter Eight: Early 1900s: When the Beast Kingdom Reached its Biblical Form?

1. "World War II: D-Day The Invasion of Normandy" Eisenhower Library, https://www.eisenhowerlibrary.gov/research/online-documents/world-war-ii-d-day-invasion-normandy

2. AZQuotes.com "Mayer Amschel Rothchild Quote"

3. "A Satanic Revolution: Major Warnings Emerge as Disney-Owned Network Releases Disturbing 'Little Demon' Cartoon, CBNNews, Billy Hallowell

4. 'The Creature from Jekyll Island' (American Opinion Publishing), p. 218

5. Andrew Jackson shuts down Second Bank of the U.S., History.com, November 16, 2009, https://www.history.com/this-day-in-history/andrew-jackson-shuts-down-second-bank-of-the-u-s

6. Andrew Jackson shuts down Second Bank of the U.S., History.com, November 16, 2009, https://www.history.com/this-day-in-history/andrew-jackson-shuts-down-second-bank-of-the-u-s

7. The Attempted Assassination of Andrew Jackson, Smithsonian Magazine, By Lorraine Boissonault, March 14, 2017, https://www.smithsonianmag.com/history/attempted-assassination-andrew-jackson-180962526/

8. The Attempted Assassination of Andrew Jackson, Smithsonian Magazine, By Lorraine Boissonault, March 14, 2017, https://www.smithsonianmag.com/history/attempted-assassination-andrew-jackson-180962526/

Chapter Nine: Revelation 13: Rapidly Being Established

1. Canadian Pastor Still in Jail After Holding Church Service for Truckers, The Epoch Times, By Alice Giordano, March 22, 2022

2. Truckers Force Ambassador Bridge shutdown over vaccine protest, New York Post, February 8, 2022

3. Banks Have Begun Freezing Accounts Linked to Truckers Protest, Newsweek, By Kathrine Fung, February 18, 2022

4. Implementation of the United Nations Legal Identity Agenda: United Nations Country Team Operations Guidelines, United Nations Statistics Division

5. Implementation of the United Nations Legal Identity Agenda: United Nations Country Team Operations Guidelines, United Nations Statistics Division

6. Implementation of the United Nations Legal Identity Agenda: United Nations Country Team Operations Guidelines, United Nations Statistics Division

7. The Most Dangerous International Treaty Ever Proposed, The Brownstone Institute via ZeroHedge.com, By Molly Kingsley, https://www.zerohedge.com/geopolitical/most-dangerous-international-treaty-ever-proposed

8. The Most Dangerous International Treaty Ever Proposed, The Brownstone Institute via ZeroHedge.com, By Molly Kingsley, https://www.zerohedge.com/geopolitical/most-dangerous-international-treaty-ever-proposed

9. Biden's Amendments Hand U.S. Sovereignty to the WHO, The Desert Review, By Liberty Counsel, May 12, 2022, https://www.thedesertreview.com/opinion/columnists/biden-s-amendments-hand-u-s-sovereignty-to-the-who/article_efcbf104-d20b-11ec-b257-b7c86410fc43.html

10. World Health Organization Power Grab, James Dobson Show, Interview with Michele Bachmann, https://www.youtube.com/watch?v=HH1CCvvLC40&t=27s

11. IMF Unveils New Global Currency Known As The "Universal Monetary Unit" To "Transform" World Economy, The Economic Collapse Blog via Zero Hedge, Michael Snyder, April 15, 2023

12. IMF Unveils New Global Currency Known As The "Universal Monetary Unit" To "Transform" World Economy, The Economic Collapse Blog via Zero Hedge, Michael Snyder, April 15, 2023

13. ECB's Lagarde gets pranked, reveals digital euro will have 'limited' control, Forkast News, April 7, 2023, https://finance.yahoo.com/news/ecb-lagarde-gets-pranked-reveals-135218145.html

14. ECB's Lagarde gets pranked, reveals digital euro will have 'limited' control, Forkast News, April 7, 2023, https://finance.yahoo.com/news/ecb-lagarde-gets-pranked-reveals-135218145.html

15. United Nations Planning Digital IN Linked to Bank Accounts," Zero Hedge, June 20, 2023, Frank Bergman via Slaynews.com

16. Watch: IMF Managing Director says "We are working hard on a global CBDC," Zero Hedge via Summit News, By Steve Watson, June 22, 2023, https://www.zerohedge.com/geopolitical/watch-imf-managing-director-says-we-are-working-hard-global-cbdc

17. "A Global Digital Compact" – UN Promoting Censorship, Social Credit, & Much More," Zero Hedge via Off-Gurdian.org, By Kit Knightly, June 23, 2023, https://www.zerohedge.com/geopolitical/global-digital-compact-un-promoting-censorship-social-cvredit-much-more

18. Ibid

19. The U.N. Is Planning to Seize Global 'Emergency' Powers With Biden's Support, The Federalist.com, By Justin Haskins, July 4, 2023, https://thefederalist.com/2023/07/04/the-u-n-is-planning-to-seize-global-emergency-powers-with-bidens-support/

20. The U.N. Is Planning to Seize Global 'Emergency' Powers With Biden's Support, The Federalist.com, By Justin Haskins, July 4, 2023, https://thefederalist.com/2023/07/04/the-u-n-is-planning-to-seize-global-emergency-powers-with-bidens-support/

21. The U.N. Is Planning to Seize Global 'Emergency' Powers With Biden's Support, The Federalist.com, By Justin Haskins, July 4, 2023, https://thefederalist.

com/2023/07/04/the-u-n-is-planning-to-seize-global-emergency-powers-w
ith-bidens-support/

Chapter Ten: Artificial Intelligence: The Beast Kingdom Supercharged

1. "'Out of control' AI is a threat to civilization," The Telegraph, By Gareth Corfield, March 29, 2023, https://www.telegraph.co.uk/business/2023/03/29/control-ai-threat-civilisation-warns-elon-musk/
2. "'Out of control' AI is a threat to civilization," The Telegraph, By Gareth Corfield, March 29, 2023, https://www.telegraph.co.uk/business/2023/03/29/control-ai-threat-civilisation-warns-elon-musk/
3. "'Out of control' AI is a threat to civilization," The Telegraph, By Gareth Corfield, March 29, 2023, https://www.telegraph.co.uk/business/2023/03/29/control-ai-threat-civilisation-warns-elon-musk/
4. "Pausing AI Development Isn't Enough. We need to Shut it All Down," Time Magazine, By Lon Tweeten, March 29, 2023
5. "Pausing AI Development Isn't Enough. We need to Shut it All Down," Time Magazine, By Lon Tweeten, March 29, 2023
6. "Pausing AI Development Isn't Enough. We need to Shut it All Down," Time Magazine, By Lon Tweeten, March 29, 2023
7. Killer AI Invented 40,000 'lethal chemical weapons" in just six hours, The Sun, By Charlotte Edwards, March 18,2022, https://www.the-sun.com/tech/4925922/killer-ai-invents-lethal-chemical-weapons/
8. Bipartisan Bill Aims to Prevent AI From Launching Nuclear Weapons, Zero Hedge via Common Dreams, By Brett Williams, May 1, 2023, https://www.zerohedge.com/markets/bipartisan-bill-aims-prevent-ai-launching-nuclear-weapons
9. What are deepfakes-and how can you spot them?, The Guardian, By Ian Sample, January 13, 2020, https://www.theguardian.com/technology/2020/jan/13/what-are-deepfakes-and-how-can-you-spot-them
10. Elon Musk Sounds the Alarm About the Dangers of AI and ChatGPT, The Street, By Luc Olinga, February 27, 2023.
11. Hacking Humanity: Transhumanism, Mises Institute, By Michael Rectenwald, April 14, 2023

Chapter Eleven: Thelemic Occult Magick

1. *The Magick of Alister Crowley: A Handbook of the Rituals of Thelema*, Lon Milo DuQuette, Weiser Classic Series
2. *New York Post*, Megan Kelly blasts 'Satanic' Sam Smith's Grammy performance, Ariel Zilber, February 7, 2023
3. *The Magick of Alister Crowley: A Handbook of the Rituals of Thelema*, Lon Milo DuQuette, Weiser Classic Series
4. *BBC News*, Georgia Guidestones: 'America's Stonehenge' demolished after blast, July 7, 2022
5. *Independent*, What are the Georgia Guidestones and where did they come from, Oliver O'Connell, July 7, 2022
6. *Independent*, What are the Georgia Guidestones and where did they come from, Oliver O'Connell, July 7, 2022
7. *Independent*, What are the Georgia Guidestones and where did they come from, Oliver O'Connell, July 7, 2022
8. *Independent*, What are the Georgia Guidestones and where did they come from, Oliver O'Connell, July 7, 2022
9. *Human Coalition*, The ABC's of the American Baby Code, Brian Fisher
10. Eye Opening Quotes from planned parenthood founder Margaret Sanger https://www.lifenews.com/2013/03/11/10-eye-opening-quotes-from-planned-parenthood-founder-margaret-sanger/
11. *Making Gay OK*, Robert R. Reilly author, Ignatius Press San Francisco, 2014
12. *Making Gay OK*, Robert R. Reilly author, Ignatius Press San Francisco, 2014
13. *Making Gay OK*, Robert R. Reilly author, Ignatius Press San Francisco, 2014
14. *Making Gay OK*, Robert R. Reilly author, Ignatius Press San Francisco, 2014
15. *New York Post*, Megan Kelly blasts 'Satanic' Sam Smith's Grammy performance, Ariel Zilber, February 7, 2023
16. The 2009 VMA's: The Occult Mega-Ritual, By Vigliant Citizen, September 25, 2009, https://vigilantcitizen.com/musicbusiness/the-2009-vmas-the-occult-mega-ritual/

Chapter Twelve: Worshiping Moloch

1. *Birmingham 2022 Commonwealth Games*, https://www.birmingham2022.com/

2. *Politico*, Foreign Affairs "King Charles is Too Political for the USA" 9/8/2022 https://www.politico.com/news/magazine/2022/09/08/king-charles-activist-unpopular-america-00055757

3. *Birmingham 2022 Commonwealth Games*, https://www.birmingham2022.com/

4. *Britannica*, "Moloch Ancient Deity," Accessed 12.14.2022 https://www.britannica.com/topic/Moloch-ancient-god

5. *Holy Bible*, Book of Deuteronomy 20:17

6. *Democracy in America*, Alexis de Tocqueville

7. Vox, "Each month, thousands of witches cast a spell against Donald Trump," October 30, 2017

Chapter Thirteen: The Beast Kingdom & the World Economic Forum

1. The COVID Blueprint: The Next Crisis' Globalists Will Use to Control You, Glenn TV, Ep 249, February 2023

2. The New York Post, The COVID Blueprint: The Next Crisis' Globalists Will Use to Control You, Glenn TV, Ep 249, February 2023

3. "Days after Nashville Shooting, Biden Condemns 'Violence against Transgender Women'," Washington Free Beacon, Ben Wilson, March 30, 2023, https://freebeacon.com/biden-administration/days-after-nashville-shooting-biden-condemns-violence-against-transgender-women/

4. Washington Examiner, Gabe Kaminsky, March 22, 2023

5. The COVID Blueprint: The Next Crisis' Globalists Will Use to Control You, Glenn TV, Ep 249, February 2023

6. Bank of England tells ministers to intervene on digital currencies 'programming' The Telegraph, Tim Wallace, June 21, 2021

7. The COVID Blueprint: The Next Crisis' Globalists Will Use to Control You, Glenn TV, Ep 249, February 2023

8. Hacking Humanity: Transhumanism, Mises Institute, By Michael Rectenwald, April 14, 2023

9. Hacking Humanity: Transhumanism, Mises Institute, By Michael Rectenwald, April 14, 2023

10. Hacking Humanity: Transhumanism, Mises Institute, By Michael Rectenwald, April 14, 2023

11. The COVID Blueprint: The Next Crisis' Globalists Will Use to Control You, Glenn TV, Ep 249, February 2023

12. The COVID Blueprint: The Next Crisis' Globalists Will Use to Control You, Glenn TV, Ep 249, February 2023

Chapter Fourteen: Barack Obama: The Manchurian President

1. The Obama Files, http://the obamafile.com/_associates/obamaassociates.htm
2. The Obama Files, http://the obamafile.com/_associates/obamaassociates.htm
3. The Obama Files, http://the obamafile.com/_associates/obamaassociates.htm
4. Jay Stone, "Obama Strategy to Win at All Costs Violated his Challengers' Civil Rights," http://stoneformayor.com/obamas-strategy-to-win-at-all-costs-violated-his-challengers-civil-rights/
5. Ibid
6. Fox News, Ryan Drops Out of Ill. Senate Race," 06/25/2004, http://www.foxnews.com/story/0,2933,123716,00.html
7. Dennis W., Free republic, "David Axelrod---Gets Obama's opponent's sealed divorce records opened up," 9/6/2008, http://www.freerepublic.com/focus/news/2075850/posts
8. Ibid
9. Steve Kornacki, New York Observer, "A Brief History of Democratic Convention Keynotes," http://observer.com/2008/08/a-brief-history-of-democratic-convention-keynoters/
10. Ibid
11. Nick Mathiason, The Guardian, "Three weeks that changed the world," http://www.guardian.co.uk/business/2008/dec/28/markets-credit-crunch-banking-2008
12. Ibid

Chapter Fifteen: Barack Obama: Servant of the Beast Kingdom

1. The Guardian, "Barack Obama, the Arab spring and a series of unforeseen events," Ian Black, October 21, 2012, https://www.theguardian.com/world/2012/oct/21/barack-obama-arab-spring-cairo-speech
2. The Guardian, "Barack Obama says Libya was 'worst mistake' of his presidency," April 11, 2016, https://www.theguardian.com/us-news/2016/apr/12/barack-obama-says-libya-was-worst-mistake-of-his-presidency

3. Foreign Policy, "Syria Will Stain Obama's Legacy Forever," D. Greenberg, December 16, 2016, https://foreignpolicy.com/2016/12/29/obama-never-understood-how-history-works/

4. "Declassified documents show security assurances against NATO expansion to Soviet leaders from Baker, Bush, Genscher, Kohl, Gates, Mitterand, Thatcher, Hurd, Major, and Woerner, http://nsarchive.gwu.edu

5. The Guardian, "It's not Russia that's pushed Ukraine to the brink of war," S. Milne, April 30, 2014, https://www.theguardian.com/commentisfree/2014/apr/30/russia-ukraine-war-kiev-conflict

6. Newsweek, "Russia Claims U.S. Ordered Ukraine to Stop Peace Talks," J. Jackson, 6/15/2022, https://www.newsweek.com/russia-claims-us-ordered-ukraine-stop-peace-talks-1716265

7. The Intercept, "Conflicting Reports Thicken Nord Stream Bombing Plot," J. Scahill, March 10, 2023, https://theintercept.com/2023/03/10/nord-stream-pipeline-bombing/

8. Slate News & Politics, "Fundamentally Transforming the United States of America," D. Weigel, October 18, 2011, https://slate.com/news-and-politics/2011/10/fundamentally-transforming-the-united-states-of-america.html

9. Billy Hallowell, "Obama Appoints Transgender Leader to Advisory Council on Faith-Based Neighborhood Partnerships," *The Blaze*, May 19, 2016. (By Wallbuilders.com)

10. Todd Starnes, "DOJ Defunds At-Risk Youth Programs over "God" Reference," *Townhall*, June 25, 2013. (By Wallbuilders.com)

11. Sheryl Gay Stolberg, "Minister Backs Out of Speech at Inaugural," *New York Times*, January 10, 2013; Eric Marrapodi, "Giglio bows out of inauguration over sermon on gays," *CNN*, January 10, 2013. (By Wallbuilders.com)

12. Audrey Hudson, "Obama administration religious service for student loan forgiveness," *Human Events*, February 15, 2012. (By Wallbuilders.com)

13. Ted Olson, "Church Wins Firing Case at Supreme Court," *Christianity Today*, January 11, 2012. . (By Wallbuilders.com)

14. Todd Starns, "Obama Administration Opposes FDR Prayer at WWII Memorial," *Fox News*, November 4, 2011. (By Wallbuilders.com)

15. "Remarks by the President at the University of Indonesia in Jakarta, Indonesia," *The White House*, November 10, 2010. (By Wallbuilders.com)

16. Johanna Neuman, "Obama end Bush-era National Prayer Day Service at White House," *Los Angeles Times*, May 7, 2009. (By Wallbuilders.com)

17. Jim Lovino, "Jesus Missing From Obama's Georgetown Speech," *NBC Washington*, April 17, 2009. .(By Wallbuilders.com)

18. Chris McGreal, "Vatican vetoes Barack Obama's nominees for U.S. Ambassador," *The Guardian*, April 14, 2009. (By Wallbuilders.com)

19. Sarah Pulliam Baily, "Obama: 'They cling to guns or religion'," *Christianity Today*, April 13, 2008. . (By Wallbuilders.com)

20. Todd Starnes, "Boykin bounced: Fort Riley cancels Delta Force hero's prayer breakfast speech," *Fox News*, June 2, 2016. (By Wallbuilders.com)

21. Debra Heine, "USAF Vet Forcibly Removed from Flag-Folding Ceremony for Mentioning God," *PJMedia*, June 20, 2016. (By Wallbuilders.com)

22. Steven Ertelt, "Army Briefing Tells Soldiers Christians and Pro-Lifers are a "Radical" Threat," *LifeNews*, October 23, 2013. (By Wallbuilders.com)

23. "Military gives bonuses only to same-sex couples," *WND*, August 20, 2013. (By Wallbuilders.com)

24. Melanie Korb, "Air Force Invites Drag Queens to Perform on 'Diversity Day'," *Charisma News*, August 19, 2013. (By Wallbuilders.com)

25. Todd Starnes, "Obama 'Strongly Objects' to Religious Liberty Amendment," *Townhall*, June 12, 2013. (By Wallbuilders.com)

26. Todd Starnes, "Air Force Officer Told to Remove Bible from Desk," *Townhall. com*, May 3, 2013. (By Wallbuilders.com)

27. Jack Minor, "Military Warned 'evangelicals' No. 1 Threat," *WND*, April 5, 2013. (By Wallbuilders.com)

28. Jenny Dean, "Air Force Academy adapts to pagans, druids, witches and Wiccans," *Los Angeles Times*, November 26, 2011. (By Wallbuilders.com)

Chapter Sixteen: Hitler's Third Reich: Bringing the Beast to America

1. History Extra, "Witches, werewolves and vampires: The Nazi's quest for the supernatural," HistoryExtra.com, July 29, 2021, https://www.historyextra. com/period/20th-century/nazi-supernatural-ideology-witches-werewolves-vampires/

2. Ibid

3. Washington Post, "It turns out 'Raiders of the Lost Ark' wasn't so far off," Aug 2, 2017, https://www.google.com/search?q=Nazi+Occult&oq=Nazi+Occult&aqs=chrome..69i57j35i39.4361j0j15&sourceid=chrome&ie=UTF-8#ip=1

4. Military History Now, "Otto Rahn – Meet the Nazi 'Indiana Jones' Behind the Third Reich's Hunt for the Holy Grail," November 21, 2020, https://militaryhistorynow.com/2020/11/21/otto-rahn-meet-the-nazi-indiana-jones-behind-the-third-reichs-hunt-for-the-holy-grail/

5. History Extra, "Witches, werewolves and vampires: The Nazi's quest for the supernatural," HistoryExtra.com, July 29, 2021, https://www.historyextra.com/period/20th-century/nazi-supernatural-ideology-witches-werewolves-vampires/

6. Ibid

7. Military History Now, "Lucky Bastard! – Seven Times Adolf Hitler Cheated Death," David Lawlor, May 11, 2017, https://militaryhistorynow.com/2017/05/11/lucky-bastard-seven-times-hitler-narrowly-escaped-death/

8. Ibid

9. Ibid

10. Ibid

11. Ibid

12. On The Front Tours, "Nazi Temple of Doom – The Real Castle," June 23, 2020, https://onthefront.com/blog/2020/6/23/nazi-temple-of-doom-the-real-castle-wolfenstein

13. NPR, "How Thousands of Nazi's Were rewarded with life in the U.S.," Terry Gross, November 5, 2014

14. The New York Times, "In Cold War, U.S. Spy Agencies Used 1,000 Nazis, Eric Lichtblau, Oct. 26, 2014

15. CATO Institute, "America's Ukraine Hypocrisy, August 6, 2017, https://www.cato.org/commentary/americas-ukraine-hypocrisy

16. BBC, "Grave of top Nazi leader Reinhard Heydrich opened in Berlin," December 16, 2019, https://www.bbc.com/news/world-europe-50806873

17. Experience History, Nazi Temple of Doom – The real Castle Wolfenstein, June 23, 2020, https://onthefront.com/blog/2020/6/23/nazi-temple-of-doom-the-real-castle-wolfenstein

18. Experience History, Nazi Temple of Doom – The real Castle Wolfenstein, June 23, 2020, https://onthefront.com/blog/2020/6/23/nazi-temple-of-doom-the-real-castle-wolfenstein

Chapter Seventeen: Operation Paperclip: A Deal with the Devil

1. Operation Paperclip: The Secret Intelligence Program that Brought Nazi Scientists to America, Author Anna Jacobson, Little, Brown and Company, 2.11.2014
2. Operation Paperclip: The Secret Intelligence Program that Brought Nazi Scientists to America, Author Anna Jacobson, Little, Brown and Company, 2.11.2014
3. New York Times, "In Cold War, U.S. Spy Agencies used 1,000 Nazis" Eric Lichtblau, October 14, 2014
4. New York Times, "In Cold War, U.S. Spy Agencies used 1,000 Nazis" Eric Lichtblau, October 14, 2014
5. New York Times, "In Cold War, U.S. Spy Agencies used 1,000 Nazis" Eric Lichtblau, October 14, 2014
6. National Public Radio, "How Thousands of Nazis Were Rewarded with life in the U.S., Terry Gross Interview of Eric Lichtblau, November 5, 2014
7. National Public Radio, "How Thousands of Nazis Were Rewarded with life in the U.S., Terry Gross Interview of Eric Lichtblau, November 5, 2014

Chapter Eighteen: Who is the Antichrist?

Chapter Nineteen: Mushroom Clouds-Heavenly Wonders & "Peace"

Chapter Twenty: When Trojan Horses Attack

Epilogue: When Trojan Horses Attack